WINSTON CHURCHILL

HIS LIFE AS A PAINTER

WINSTON
CHURCHILL

HIS LIFE AS A PAINTER

*

A Memoir by his Daughter
MARY SOAMES

With a Foreword by Derek Hill

VIKING

VIKING

Published by the Penguin Group

Penguin Books Canada Ltd, 2801 John Street, Markham, Ontario, Canada L3R 1B4
Penguin Books Ltd, 27 Wrights Lane, London W8 5TZ, England
Viking Penguin Inc., 40 West 23rd Street, New York, New York 10010, USA
Penguin Books Australia Ltd, Ringwood, Victoria, Australia
Penguin Books (NZ) Ltd, 182–190 Wairau Road, Auckland 10, New Zealand

Penguin Books Ltd, Registered Offices: Harmondsworth, Middlesex, England

First published 1990

1 3 5 7 9 10 8 6 4 2

Printed and bound in the United Kingdom

Canadian Cataloguing in Publication Data
Soames, Mary.
Winston Churchill: his life as a painter

ISBN 0-670-83626-5

1. Churchill, Winston S. (Winston Spencer), 1874–1965.
2. Painters—Great Britain—Biography.
3. Statesmen—Great Britain—Biography.   I. Title.

ND497.C548S62 1990   759.2   C90-094228-2

Contents

List of Illustrations

The names of Winston Churchill and Clementine Churchill have been abbreviated to WSC and CSC throughout. References in parentheses are to the catalogue compiled by David Coombs, *Churchill: His Paintings* (see Select Bibliography). All paintings are in oils, and all are on canvas unless otherwise indicated.

7

BLACK-AND-WHITE ILLUSTRATIONS

Author's Preface
and Acknowledgements

I wish first of all to acknowledge my gratitude to Her Majesty The Queen for her gracious permission to reproduce the picture by my father *The Palladian Bridge at Wilton*, 1925 (p. 52), which is in Her Majesty's collection; and also her permission to quote from a letter of Her Majesty's to my father. I wish also to thank Her Majesty Queen Elizabeth The Queen Mother, and Her Royal Highness The Princess Margaret, Countess of Snowdon, for their gracious permission to quote excerpts from letters they wrote to my father.

I am most grateful to Derek Hill whose advice in the selection of Winston Churchill's pictures for reproduction in the book has been invaluable and paramount. He has given so much of his valuable time and thought both to myself and to my publishers, not only in choosing the pictures but also in helping to verify the colour quality of the reproductions, and I thank him most warmly.

The only catalogue to date of Winston Churchill's paintings was compiled in 1966 by David Coombs (now the Editor of the *Antique Collector*); *Churchill: His Paintings* which was designed and produced by George Rainbird Ltd, and published by Hamish Hamilton, London, in 1967. David Coombs also wrote the introduction to the catalogue. This work has proved invaluable to me; and I wish to thank Mr Coombs also for his ready personal help, particularly in the matter of ascribing dates with reasonable accuracy to the pictures chosen. Winston Churchill did not keep records of the pictures he painted, and although, of course, many of them date themselves by their subjects or context, many can only be dated by their similarity of subject or style, or by the influence they reflect of artists who are known to have helped to form Churchill's technique at various times. It is here that David Coombs's advice has been vital to my attempts to date the pictures. In a few cases the dates or subjects attributed to the pictures shown here are not the same as in Coombs's *Churchill: His Paintings*: this is because I have had the advantage of various sources not available to David Coombs at the time, such as letters, later publications, and personal knowledge.

I have based the factual account of events in my father's life on his official biography: *Winston S. Churchill* by Martin Gilbert, published by Heinemann (London); and I have drawn copiously on the letters and documents which appear in the Companion Volumes to the biography (which for the time being cease in 1939). I am most grateful to Martin Gilbert for his ready assistance at all times, not only in answering various queries, but also in drawing my attention to several items from the Churchill Papers which were not to be found in the Companion Volumes.

I wish to thank C & T Publications Ltd for permission to quote from the official biography of Winston S. Churchill (including the Companion Volumes) by Martin Gilbert, and my nephew, Winston S. Churchill, MP, for permission to use material from the Randolph Churchill Papers, and copyright material from the writings of Sir Winston Churchill. My thanks are also due to the Trustees for permission to use material from the Archive Settlement Trust.

The papers of my mother, Baroness Spencer-Churchill, GBE, are deposited at Churchill College, Cambridge (Spencer-Churchill Papers), which owns the copyright. I am grateful to Correlli Barnett, MA, the Keeper of the Churchill Archives Centre for permission to quote from these Papers.

I am grateful to The Churchill Heritage Ltd in which is vested the copyright of the great majority of Winston Churchill's pictures, and with whose active cooperation this book of mine is produced, for permission to reproduce the paintings illustrated here. I wish to thank most warmly my cousin, Peregrine S. Churchill, the Company's Managing Director, for all his help and advice, from the earliest beginnings of this project to its final fulfilment.

I am greatly indebted to the following members of my family and other individuals who have allowed us to photograph and reproduce Churchill pictures in their possession: The Countess of Avon; Peregrine S. Churchill; Winston S. Churchill, MP; Mrs Arabella Churchill-MacLeod; Lady Margaret Colville; Viscount Cranborne; Miss Geraldine Fairfax-Cholmeley; The Rt. Hon. Edward Heath, MBE, MP; the late Norman G. Hickman, DSC; The Countess Peel; Hon. Mrs Celia Perkins; Mr and Mrs Russell S. Reynolds Jnr; the Marquess of Salisbury; Hon. Julian Sandys, QC; Anne, Duchess of Westminster. And for permission to reproduce the drawing of Oscar Nemon, I wish to thank Mr F. Bartlett Watt.

I am grateful to the Royal Academy of Arts for permission to reproduce Winston Churchill's Diploma Work *Cap d'Ail, Alpes Maritimes, 1952* (p. 185); and to the Trustees of the Tate Gallery for permission to reproduce *The Loup River, Alpes Maritimes, 1936* (p. 116).

My warm thanks are due to the National Trust for permission to reproduce Churchill pictures in their possession at Chartwell. And I am particularly grateful to Mrs Jean Broome, the Administrator at Chartwell, and her assistants for their ready help on so many occasions.

I wish to thank the following people who in various ways have helped me: Hon. Philip Astor for sending me letters from my father to his grandfather, Colonel John Astor (later first Lord Astor of Hever); Lady Margaret Myddelton for her recollections of her stepfather, Colonel John Astor, and my father; Dr Wendy Baron for talking to me about Sickert and his painting techniques; Duncan McLaren and David Ellis-Jones for information concerning the Galerie Druet in Paris; Kenneth Rose for his recollections and the account in his diary of my father and R. A. Butler painting together; Sir Roy Strong and Michael J. B. Mills, the Managing Agent of the Sutton Place Foundation, for supplying the winning clues in my search for the correct identification of the picture on p. 53; Irene, Lady Astor of Hever, the Hon. Lady Cazalet, The Earl of Pembroke, Anne, Duchess of Westminster, and The Duke of Westminster, for their assistance in identifying the subjects of certain pictures; Ms Eileen Coffman, Manager of Visual Resources of the Dallas Museum of Art, for helping me trace the whereabouts of a picture; Warren M. Hollrah, Archivist at the Winston Churchill Memorial and Library in the United States, Westminster College, Fulton, Missouri, for much useful information about Churchill pictures in the Library and elsewhere in the USA; the Hon. Edwina Sandys for help and encouragement; and Wylma Wayne for her continued help in tracing pictures.

The following people have taken time and trouble to answer various queries, and I am truly grateful to them: Miss M. M. Beveridge, Registrar of Churchill College, Cambridge; the County Archivists at the East Sussex, the West Sussex and the Surrey County Record Offices; Paul Duffie, the Administrator at Blenheim Palace; B. A. King, Librarian of the Rugby Football Union; Ms Laura Lambert, Secretary to the Royal Society of Portrait Painters.

The author and publishers are grateful to the following authors, publishers, agents, literary executors and others for permission to quote copyright material not already mentioned: Mark Birley for use of a memorandum from his father, Sir Oswald Birley; Fleur Cowles to quote from her book *An Artist's Journey*; Henry Lessore to publish two letters from Walter Sickert; Mrs Jessie Maze to publish letters written by her late husband Paul Maze; Falcon Nemon Stuart to use excerpts from his father Oscar Nemon's letters and papers, and to reproduce Churchill's pencil sketch; Viscount Norwich to use extracts from Lady Diana Cooper's letters to Conrad Russell; Sir

John Rothenstein to quote from his autobiography *Time's Thievish Progress* and from *Churchill: A Tribute by various hands, on his Eightieth Birthday* (Cassell, 1955); Peter Quennell to quote from *The Wanton Chase*; The Lady Sempill to quote from her grandfather Sir John Lavery's letters; F. Bartlett Watt for making available to me extracts from letters and papers of Oscar Nemon; Constable Publishers to quote from *Winston Churchill: The Struggle For Survival 1940–65* by Lord Moran; Hamish Hamilton and Viking Press to quote from *Maxine* by Diana Forbes-Robertson; Hodder & Stoughton to quote from *The Fringes of Power* by Sir John Colville; Methuen, London, to quote from *Future Indefinite* by Noel Coward; Peters Fraser & Dunlop to quote from *Between the Thunder and the Sun* by Vincent Sheean.

We have had difficulty in contacting several copyright holders (chiefly in books published many years ago and now out of print). Where we have failed in this, we offer our sincere apologies, and thank them for 'permission' we have ventured to assume.

In order to achieve a high standard of colour reproduction, most of the pictures selected for this book were photographed by Gordon Robertson of A. C. Cooper Ltd, to whom I extend my thanks for his skill and care.

The index has been compiled by Douglas Matthews, the Librarian of the London Library, and I am most grateful to him.

I have been delighted to collaborate once again with Collins, and I wish to thank most warmly Carol O'Brien and Amanda McCardie my editors; and Ronald Clark, who has designed the book with such meticulous care. Their enthusiasm and painstaking zeal to achieve a high standard has made the enterprise a most inspiring one for me.

Once again it gives me pleasure to acknowledge the help of Ann Hoffmann, who has most kindly read and corrected the manuscript and checked the galley proofs. I greatly value her keen eye and good advice.

Finally my heartfelt thanks to Nonie Chapman, my secretary, who has word-processed my type/hand script, organized endless lists of pictures and sources, written countless letters, and kept the rest of my life on an even keel – all with unfailing cheerfulness and unflagging energy.

Castle Mill House, Hampshire
Sloane Court West, London

MARY SOAMES
April 1990

In all letters and documents quoted the original spelling has been retained; some punctuation has been amended slightly for ease of comprehension.

FOREWORD

Winston Churchill
Honorary Academician Extraordinary

When I visited the annual Summer Exhibition of the Royal Academy at Burlington House I never bought a catalogue until I had been round the galleries for the first time; I marked down on paper the numbers of the pictures I liked best, and only later looked in the catalogue to see who had painted them. There was always a picture by Winston Churchill – often, I seem to remember, of water with stony banks and overhanging trees. Certainly *The Loup River* (p. 116), now owned by the Tate Gallery, must have been one of them, and for this reason I never thought of Churchill as a mere amateur painter, any more than Lord Duveen did when he, with Kenneth Clark and Oswald Birley, once judged an exhibition of anonymous amateur artists. The obvious winner, chosen by all three judges, had painted such a strong and masterly picture that Duveen at first refused to acknowledge that the artist could possibly be an amateur. *Winter sunshine, Chartwell*, (p. 58) painted in around 1924, was the work of a fine artist, regardless of the category in which he might be placed.

A little book that Churchill first published in 1948, called *Painting as a Pastime*, could equally have been called *Painting as a Pleasure*, and neither title would of necessity mean that the artist was an amateur. Any painter could admit that his work was both a pastime and a pleasure. Probably it ought to be both. The fact that a large number of paintings by Churchill could not be selected as worthy of a book is again in no way surprising; it is a pity that a far more selective process does not apply to the reproduction of works by some artists considered today to be of a high standard. Many artists destroy the works they don't wish to pass on to posterity. It seems that Churchill did not do this, but merely stacked away the hundreds of paintings he managed to fit into an already overcrowded lifetime. That Churchill was a great national leader and can still be considered as an artist should be no more surprising than that Rubens was an Ambassador of his country and at the same time one of the most prolific artists that ever lived.

I am not comparing the two artists in any way. Churchill was never

13

interested in depicting heroic or biblical scenes of antiquity, and Rubens produced all too few pure landscapes. Rubens excelled as a portraitist; Churchill did not. His chief concern was to paint the landscapes that, in whatever country he may have found them, gave him peace and tranquillity of mind – an escape, even, from the world he had to help control, and to assist in its struggle for survival.

Churchill records that it was Lady Lavery who first gave him a lesson by seizing his tentative brush: 'Splash into the turpentine, wallop into the blue and the white, frantic flourish on the palette – clean no longer – and then several large fierce strokes and slashes of blue on the absolutely cowering canvas'. It was probably this early lesson in attack that helped Churchill to avoid being a mere 'amateur'. Sickert told Churchill to 'put on the paint as though you were scraping your feet on a door-mat'. Neither of these approaches are reminiscent of the amateur works of maiden aunts (though the latter certainly had in common with Churchill a love of what they saw, scrutinized and wished to remember when their works were taken home).

In the selection of pictures for this book we have tried to choose at least one landscape from each of Churchill's favourite places. Several of them bring back a nostalgic wave of memory, like the steps down to Lake Como at Menaggio where I so often walked down to bathe, or the pool at the Villa Zoraïdes on Cap Martin, with the Capponcina nearby, where I painted some of my own first landscapes in the thirties. Landscapes, and especially impressionist pictures of them, are so often able to record exact moments of pleasure at seeing and feeling some climatic variation – whether in the sky or on the sea or land beneath – and Churchill always tried to capture these moments of exhilaration when freed from affairs of state.

Constable said that 'a self-taught artist is one taught by a very ignorant man'. Certainly there are notable influences on Churchill's work; there were many artist friends who inspired and encouraged him – Sickert, Lavery, Nicholson, and Maze among them. An early self-portrait is reminiscent of Daumier, while some of the dark, overhung river scenes recall a certain period in the work of Segonzac – who was also one of Churchill's acquaintances of many years. And he copied pictures by both Sargent and Daubigny.

What is immediately attractive in Churchill's pictures is his obvious love of paint and brush. The texture of paint is all-important to him, and when I once asked to see some Churchill drawings I learned that there were none; he just drew with his brushes and knew exactly how thick or thin the paint application should be for the surface or subject he was representing. Many artists of today can draw superbly, but when they turn to oil paintings merely transfer their drawings on to canvas in colour, oblivious to the possibilities of paint texture. Others do use the paint, colour and texture, but underneath have none of the drawing ability so necessary to control the surface bravura. To be a painter who does not relish the possibilities of actual pigment in paint is to be like a stained-glass artist who uses only linear glass with no colour, missing the whole point of light shining through the jewel-like transparency.

Churchill obviously revelled in what he was doing when he painted, and ably carried his histrionic sense of battle into his world of art. He seemed to have no hesitations and no inhibitions.

The pictures Mary Soames and I have selected for reproduction in this book are ones that especially appeal to me as a fellow painter. The land-scapes, for instance, need not be the prettiest he did nor even the most attractive, but they have a painterly quality that transcends mere amateurish charm. Others in our selection have been included primarily for their strong historical interest. But they are all, we think, pictures that will live, and will always command respect.

DEREK HILL
October 1989

Possibly the earliest photograph of WSC painting, and probably taken at
Hoe Farm in the summer of 1915. He is watched by CSC in a sun bonnet.
Courtesy of Peregrine Churchill

CHAPTER ONE

To have reached the age of forty without ever handling a brush or fiddling with a pencil, to have regarded with mature eye the painting of pictures of any kind as a mystery, to have stood agape before the chalk of the pavement artist, and then suddenly to find oneself plunged in the middle of a new and intense form of interest and action with paints and palettes and canvases, and not be discouraged by results, is an astonishing and enriching experience.[1]

Thus wrote Winston Churchill a few years after he had started out on his long and happy love-affair with painting. So often with hindsight one is able to detect early signs in someone of a later-to-be-developed talent or characteristic: as a child Winston had a marvellous collection of lead soldiers, and he would spend hours on the nursery floor disposing his toy forces – the soldier, the strategist in the making. Bad as he was as a schoolboy at his books in general, yet some of his masters perceived in him a relish for the English language, and an imaginative interest in history. His capacity to learn by heart in his schooldays stored up for him a larder of prose and verse which was to enrich him (and others) for all his long life. It is true that in 1895, aged twenty-one, while he was in Cuba during the Insurrection, he had written a series of dispatches for the *Daily Graphic*; referring to them later, Churchill said he had also illustrated them. When published, however, they were signed T. C. Crowther; presumably the sketches were fairly primitive, and were redrawn for publication.[2] Later on, in a lifetime of correspondence with Clementine, his wife, he was wont to adorn his signature with 'Pugs' or 'Pigs' (according to which synonym he was affecting at the moment); these gargoyle-like creatures are charming, but one would be hard pressed to see in them artistic portents.

As he himself wrote, nothing in his life's experience had presaged that, hidden within him – perhaps crowded out by his other talents and ambitions – lay an artistic seed waiting to be called to life. And the circumstances in his career which provided the 'kick-start' to the discovery and pursuit of this new talent were among the most dramatic and disastrous of Winston Churchill's long public life, which spanned over half a century.

The spring of 1915 saw the launching of the strategic enterprise to seize Constantinople by the forcing of the Dardanelles straits, between the Turkish mainland and the Gallipoli peninsula; the naval forces being backed up by a military force which would take and hold the peninsula. This dynamic concept to provide an alternative to the horrors and immobility of trench-warfare, which now grasped Western Europe from the Channel ports to the Swiss frontier in its iron fist, had as its principal instigator and champion Winston Churchill, First Lord of the Admiralty in Asquith's Liberal Government. The operation had begun in late February 1915 with the bombardment of the outer defences of the Dardanelles.

This is not the place to recount the grievous course of the Dardanelles campaign; it is enough to say that a series of dire errors of judgement both by the War Council in London and by the commanders on the scene of action combined to ruin a brilliant strategic conception which, had it succeeded, might have dramatically shortened the course of a bloody world war. As the campaign lurched from crisis to crisis, some of those who had been strong in support of the plan now voiced doubts and criticisms, while those who had always opposed it could feel justified. Churchill, both as the foremost protagonist of the idea and as First Lord of the Admiralty, was deeply involved in details of the campaign and shouldered a heavy burden of responsibility.

At this period of the war, the Dardanelles campaign was not the only source of bad news. In France, the second Battle of Ypres at the end of April had seen the first use by the Germans of poison gas; there was a shortage of shells, and this 'scandal' was heartily fanned in the press, not only involving Lord Kitchener (a public hero), but also casting blame on the Liberal government as a whole. There had been since the beginning of the war a truce between the political parties, but the mounting tale of bad news made many Conservatives restive, and as the tidings from the Dardanelles continued to be a source of anxiety, their criticisms and hostility became principally focused upon Winston Churchill – whom they had long abhorred as a renegade Tory, and whose judgement they mistrusted. The sudden resignation of the First Sea Lord, Admiral Lord Fisher, on 15 May, as a protest against the conduct of the Dardanelles campaign, brought the simmering political crisis to boiling point.

The result of the revolt of the Conservative opposition was the formation of a coalition government under the continued leadership of Mr Asquith. Part of the price to be paid for the support of the Conservatives was the removal of Churchill from the Admiralty. He became Chancellor of the Duchy of Lancaster – an appointment with no departmental responsibility – but he still remained a member of the War Council.

The mortification felt by Churchill at his demotion was doubly painful, for he sensed that the Prime Minister, a friend and colleague of many years, had sacrificed him without a fight to the demands of the Conservatives. In leaving the Admiralty Churchill was instantly deprived of the exercise of executive power, while retaining an involvement in and a heavy responsibility for the Dardanelles campaign, in which he still believed wholeheartedly, and which he was convinced could be retrieved, even now, by strong and decisive action.

Many years later Clementine Churchill was to tell Winston's biographer, Martin Gilbert, that, looking back over all the events and crises through which they had both lived, and in which Winston had played a major part, none had been so searing as the drawn-out campaign of the Dardanelles, with its heavy toll of life and bitter aftermath. She told Martin Gilbert: 'I thought he would die of grief.'

When war broke out in 1914 Winston was forty. He and Clementine, some ten years younger, had been married for six years, and had two children: Diana, who was five, and Randolph, who was three. In October 1914 their third child, Sarah, was born at Admiralty House, then the official residence of the First Lord of the Admiralty. Their own house in Eccleston Square was let, so when Winston left the Admiralty at the end of May 1915 the Churchills were homeless. A kindly cousin, Lord Wimborne, lent them his house in Arlington Street while they rearranged their domestic affairs.

Jack Churchill, Winston's younger brother, was serving in Gallipoli as a major on the staff of the army commander, Major General Sir Ian Hamilton. Jack's wife Goonie* and their two sons John George, aged six, and two-year-old Peregrine were living at 41 Cromwell Road, South Kensington. With Jack away from home, this house was rather too big. Both families were feeling hard-up and, since the two sisters-in-law were very fond of each other, it was decided after due consultation that the 'Winstons' and the 'Jacks' should join forces in Number 41, amalgamating their nurseries under the command of one nanny.

At the end of May, Winston and Clementine had rented a charming house, Hoe Farm, near Godalming in Surrey, as a country retreat; and to this haven, with its pleasant garden, they retired at the weekends during those dreadful summer months of 1915 to lick their wounds.

---

* Born Lady Gwendeline Bertie, daughter of the seventh Earl of Abingdon.

Winston Churchill has described in vivid and moving terms his feelings at that time:

> When I left the Admiralty at the end of May, 1915, I still remained a member of the Cabinet and of the War Council. In this position I knew everything and could do nothing. The change from the intense executive activities of each day's work at the Admiralty to the narrowly measured duties of a counsellor left me gasping. Like a sea-beast fished up from the depths, or a diver too suddenly hoisted, my veins threatened to burst from the fall in pressure. I had great anxiety and no means of relieving it; I had vehement convictions and small power to give effect to them. I had to watch the unhappy casting-away of great opportunities, and the feeble execution of plans which I had launched and in which I heartily believed. I had long hours of utterly unwonted leisure in which to contemplate the frightful unfolding of the War. At a moment when every fibre of my being was inflamed to action, I was forced to remain a spectator of the tragedy, placed cruelly in a front seat. And then it was that the Muse of Painting came to my rescue – out of charity and out of chivalry, because after all she had nothing to do with me – and said, 'Are these toys any good to you? They amuse some people!'[3]

Goonie and her boys often joined Winston, Clementine and their trio at Hoe Farm. One June day as she sat in the garden sketching with watercolours, Winston wandered by deep in thought. He watched her for a few minutes, then borrowed her brush and tried his hand; Goonie was enchanted by his interest. Purloining John George's painting box, she encouraged Winston to paint a picture: the Muse had cast her spell! Very soon, Winston decided that he must further these first essays by experimenting with oils. Clementine, who like Goonie was entirely delighted with this distraction from Winston's dark broodings, rushed off to Godalming and bought whatever oil paints she could lay her hands upon; she omitted, however, to acquire any turpentine, and a period of puzzlement and frustration ensued. Help was fortunately at hand: the Churchill's close neighbours in London at 5 Cromwell Place were John Lavery, the celebrated painter, and his beautiful and also artistically gifted wife Hazel. As soon as they heard of Winston's new interest they leapt into action.

On his expeditions to London to attend the House or Dardanelles Committee, Winston bought the various items of equipment necessary for a painter – an easel, a mahogany palette, brushes, paints and turpentine. But the next step seemed difficult, as he contemplated with unaccustomed

1. *The garden at Hoe Farm, summer 1915.* Lady Gwendeline Churchill is in the foreground.
Collection: Mr Peregrine Churchill

2. *Portrait of John Lavery in his studio, 1915.* Found in Lavery's studio at the time of
his death in 1940, this painting has recently come to light through Miss Fairfax-Cholmeley,
who inherited it from her aunt Katherine Fitzgerald, Lavery's private secretary
and executor. Collection: Miss Geraldine Fairfax-Cholmeley;
on loan to the National Trust, Chartwell

nervousness the blameless whiteness of a new canvas. He started with the sky – it was on that occasion blue – and later described how

> very gingerly I mixed a little blue paint on the palette with a very small brush, and then with infinite precaution made a mark about as big as a bean upon the affronted snow-white shield. It was a challenge, a deliberate challenge; but so subdued, so halting, indeed so cataleptic, that it deserved no response. At that moment the loud approaching sound of a motor-car was heard in the drive. From this chariot there stepped swiftly and lightly none other than the gifted wife of Sir John Lavery. 'Painting! But what are you hesitating about? Let me have a brush – the big one.' Splash into the turpentine, wallop into the blue and the white, frantic flourish on the palette – clean no longer – and then several large, fierce strokes and slashes of blue on the absolutely cowering canvas. Anyone could see that it could not hit back. No evil fate avenged the jaunty violence. The canvas grinned in helplessness before me. The spell was broken. The sickly inhibitions rolled away. I seized the largest brush and fell upon my victim with Berserk fury. I have never felt any awe of a canvas since.[4]

Winston was lucky indeed to have such gifted mentors as John and Hazel Lavery to guide his earliest brushstrokes, and what had been a pleasing acquaintance now grew into a warm and lasting friendship.

Hoe Farm, both inside and out, provided his first subjects, but when he was in London Winston started to spend as much time as he could in John Lavery's studio, painting alongside him. Lavery opened up new vistas for his unusual pupil: landscapes, interiors, even portraits – a bold step for a beginner. The portrait Winston painted of John Lavery at his easel in 1915 must have been among his first, and those who can still remember John Lavery say that it is a striking likeness. Winston gave the picture to Lavery, who lent it for exhibition in 1919 to the Royal Society of Portrait Painters – this was the first time one of Winston's works was exhibited. He also painted a self-portrait which is very similar in style to the painting he did of Lavery; it is not dated, but clearly belongs to that early period of his painting. These earliest portraits show the enterprising spirit with which Winston attacked a most difficult aspect of his new-found occupation.

John Lavery later gave his opinion of his unusual pupil's talents in his autobiography:

> I know few amateur wielders of the brush with a keener sense of light and colour, or a surer grasp of essentials. I am able to prove this from experience. We have often stood up to the same motif, and in spite

of my trained eye and knowledge of possible difficulties, he with his characteristic fearlessness and freedom from convention, has time and again shown me how I should do things. Had he chosen painting instead of statesmanship I believe he would have been a great master with the brush, and as P.R.A. would have given stimulus to the Art world.[5]

But this new and riveting employment was only a spasmodic distraction from the dire course of events. The campaign in Gallipoli went from bad to worse, the Coalition government was proving as ineffective a war-machine as its predecessor, and the reconstructed Dardanelles Committee was too large for decisive action. In early August the attack at Suvla Bay by British forces was a failure resulting in both heavy casualties on the hard-fought beaches, and political repercussions detrimental to our cause, in Greece and the Balkans.

In these months Churchill ever held in his mind the thought of resignation from the Government. He was a major in the Oxfordshire Yeomanry, and an honourable door was open to him: he could join his regiment in France. Indeed at the end of October he had tendered his resignation to the Prime Minister, but Asquith had persuaded him to stay on. The only consideration which held him from this course was the feeling that he could still influence the campaign in which from its beginning he had been closely involved. In November 1915 the Cabinet decided to reduce the size of the Dardanelles Committee in the hope of making it more effective; the smaller team did not include Churchill, although he remained in the Cabinet. The one condition that had enabled him to accept the Chancellorship of the Duchy of Lancaster had now disappeared. On 11 November Churchill wrote again to the Prime Minister, and from this letter of resignation there was to be no going back. 'I could not', he wrote, 'accept a position of general responsibility for war policy without any effective share in its guidance & control . . . Nor do I feel in times like these able to remain in well-paid inactivity . . .'[6]

A week later, Major Churchill left for France, and was posted to the 2nd Battalion of the Grenadier Guards in the battle-line near Laventie. In his first letters home to Clementine he told her of the sense of happiness and content he felt, despite the dangers and the rigours of trench life: 'I did not know what release from care meant,'[7] he wrote.

Winston served with the Grenadiers until the New Year, and after a short leave, spent in London with Clementine and the children, he was appointed Colonel of the 6th Battalion, Royal Scots Fusiliers, which was resting in the village of Moolenacker (not far from Armentières), recouping its strength after heavy losses in action. Winston threw himself into this new job with zest; he found the details of military life absorbing and gave himself over entirely to the daily affairs of his battalion. Only Clementine knew of any bitterness he felt in his heart for the politicians at home, or of any repining for involvement and power on the political scene. 'I do not ever show anything but a smiling face to the military world: a proper complete detachment & contentment. But so it is a relief to write one's heart out to you . . . ,' he wrote on 10 January 1916.[8] Clementine was not only the trusted and sympathetic recipient of his confidences, she was also a perceptive informant concerning political personalities and affairs on the home front. Winston and Clementine's letters to each other during the four months he was to be at the front form a deeply moving correspondence.

When Churchill and the 6th Battalion moved up into the line once more towards the end of January 1916, they were near a village just over the Belgian frontier called Ploegsteert – instantly renamed 'Plugstreet' by the Tommies. As Battalion Commander, Churchill would operate from Support HQ at a former hospice and the Advance Battalion HQ at Laurence Farm. 'In fact,' he wrote to Clementine,

> I shall only move back about 3/4s of a mile from the front line when we are in support and supposed to be 'resting'. Therefore for the next 2 or 3 months we shall all dwell continuously in close range of the enemy's artillery.[9]

During these winter-to-spring months each normal tour of duty in the frontline trenches lasted six days. During slack periods Winston painted several pictures of the desolate scene around him at Plugstreet and Laurence Farm. Just before they went into the trenches, Colonel Churchill gave some advice to his officers (most of them very young, since nearly all the Battalion's regular officers had been killed in action). 'War is a game that is played with a smile,' he told them, adding, 'If you can't smile, grin . . .' And it may have had a steadying and encouraging effect on his soldiers to observe their Commanding Officer painting the stricken scene with deep concentration, unmoved by desultory shell-bursts in the vicinity. One of his officers, Edmund Hakewill Smith, then aged twenty-four* described how

> Winston started painting the second or third time he went up to the farm. Each time we were in the line he spent some time on his paintings. Gradually, too, the courtyard became more pitted with shellholes. As his painting came nearer to completion, he became morose, angry, and exceedingly difficult to talk to. After five or six days in this mood,

* After a gallant and distinguished career in two world wars he would become Sir Edmund, Constable and Lieutenant-Governor of Windsor Castle.

3. *Laurence Farm, 'Plugstreet', Advance Battalion HQ, early 1916.* The seated
figure reading a newspaper is WSC's second-in-command Major Sir Archibald Sinclair
(later Lord Thurso and Leader of the Liberal Party). Collection: Winston S. Churchill, MP

4. *'Plugstreet' under shell-fire, early 1916.* Collection: The National Trust, Chartwell

he suddenly appeared cheerful and delighted, like a small boy at school. I asked him what had happened, and he said 'I have been worried because I couldn't get the shell-hole right in the painting. However I did it, it looked like a mountain, but yesterday I discovered that if I put a little bit of white in it, it looked like a hole after all.[10]

When Winston knew he would have a week's leave at the beginning of March, he wrote detailed instructions to Clementine as to how the precious days and hours should be planned. 'You must parcel out the days as well as possible. I will have one dinner at my mother's, at least 3 at home, 2 plays alone with you & one man's dinner out somewhere.'[11] She was further instructed to 'work in all my friends' and one whole day was to be kept for painting in John Lavery's studio.

During those desolate winter months while Winston was in Flanders, Clementine, although consumed with anxiety (like so many thousands at that time) for her husband's safety, was driving herself hard with the organization of a network of canteens for munition workers in the north London area. Contrary to the current of her unsocial nature, she moreover forced herself to go about in political circles so that she could fuel Winston's insatiable need for news of all sorts. Goonie was a great confidante, and John and Hazel Lavery also proved stalwart and sympathetic friends; Clementine would often slip across the road in the evenings after a long day's work and sit in John Lavery's studio. He painted a moving picture of her at this time, which conveys a feeling of her fatigue and sadness.

All the time Churchill was at the front he kept in touch with the political situation at home, both through Clementine and through friends and former colleagues. During his spell of leave in March he once more immersed himself in his true element, politics, and decided to take part in the debate on Naval Estimates which took place while he was in London. His intervention proved highly controversial, but the result of his re-establishing his political contacts was to confirm in his own mind the conviction that had been growing for some little while, that his proper place was in Parliament, where policy questions of major import to the conduct of the war were being debated, and where he believed he had a vital and even unique role to play: nor was he alone in this view.

When he returned to Belgium at the end of his leave Winston had firmly formulated the intention of returning to the home front as soon as an appropriate moment presented itself; meanwhile he continued to go in and out of the line with his battalion. Letters from home brought news and differing views on what his right action should be; and mental and spiritual tension is very clearly revealed in Winston's and Clementine's letters to each other during those spring months of 1916. Torn with conflicting thoughts about his immediate future, and living in the dreary and sordid conditions of trench warfare under the constant threat of death, Winston dreamt also of a tranquil existence; on 28 March he wrote to Clementine:

> I too feel sometimes the longing for rest & peace. So much effort, so many years of ceaseless fighting & worry, so much excitement & now this rough fierce life here under the hammer of Thor, makes my older mind turn – for the first time I think to other things than action . . . wd it not be delicious to go for a few weeks to some lovely spot in Italy or Spain & just paint & wander about together in bright warm sunlight far from the clash of arms or bray of Parliaments?[12]

Winston came briefly home again to take part in the Secret Session of the House of Commons on 25 April, returning immediately afterwards to his Battalion, which was going again into the line. But the appropriate moment for him to return to London for good soon presented itself. Owing to heavy losses in the Scots regiments several battalions were to be amalgamated and, in the reorganization of the units, Winston had to give way to a senior colonel. His connection with the Royal Scots Fusiliers thus came to a natural conclusion, and early in May 1916 he returned to England to resume his parliamentary duties.

Winston and Clementine's first weekend together after his return was spent at Blenheim Palace, the home of his first cousin Sunny, the ninth Duke of Marlborough. Blenheim was his patriarchal home: he had been born there, the grandson of the seventh Duke of Marlborough, and in 1908 he had proposed to Clementine Hozier in the lovely little Temple of Diana that looks over the great lake. All his life he would return to the splendid house, with its succeeding generations of hospitable Spencer-Churchill cousins; and at the end he would choose to lie there, close by his parents, in the churchyard at Bladon, just outside the park walls.

Planning ahead for this first weekend back in England, Winston had written to Clementine from Laurence Farm on 2 May 1916:

> If you arrange this [the Blenheim visit], please get me 3 large tubes of *thin* white . . . also 3 more canvasses: and a bottle of that poisonous solution wh cleans the paint off old canvasses.[13]

From now on canvases, easel, paints and brushes would form a regular part of Winston's travelling impedimenta.

The long weekends of pre-war days – Friday to Monday (or even Tuesday) – were an outdated luxury now, and hospitable houses within easy reach of London for hard-pressed politicians or service commanders had a special appeal. Among the welcoming hostesses was Lady Paget – Minnie – an American, and a prominent member of the Prince of Wales's set. Her husband was General Sir Arthur Paget, who commanded the forces in Ireland. Their house at Kingston Hill was not only an easy drive from London, but also had a beautiful garden; John Lavery and Winston Churchill spent pleasant hours painting there. One summer Sunday in 1916, another guest was Admiral Lord Charles Beresford, retired from the Navy. He was Conservative Unionist Member of Parliament for Portsmouth, and a year before had been one of Winston's most carping Tory critics during the Dardanelles crisis. 'Master' and 'pupil' were painting away when, as John Lavery recounts,

> a hale and hearty voice behind called out, 'Hullo! Winston, when did you begin this game?' Without turning round Winston replied, 'The day you kicked me out of the Admiralty, Lord Charles.' 'Well,' said Beresford, 'who knows? I may have saved a great Master.'

John Lavery painted a charming picture of Winston at work at his easel in Lady Paget's garden during that summer.[14]

In 1915, during the fraught months leading up to Winston's departure for the front, Lavery had already painted one portrait of him in service uniform, commissioned and presented to him by the officers of the Armoured Car Squadrons, whose development he had energetically promoted. The picture now hangs at Chartwell.

It soon became known that Winston's great new hobby was painting, and people were interested and curious as to his capabilities. George Moore,* the writer, tackled Eddie Marsh, Winston's faithful and highly distinguished Private Secretary,† as to the true talent of this political animal turned artist. Marsh recounted how at a party Moore had said to him:

> 'You're the man who'll be able to tell me – what are Winston's pictures like?' 'Well,' I replied, 'they are exactly like pictures.' This enchanted him, and he repeated it everywhere.[15]

Having resigned his commission and returned to England for good, Winston threw himself into politics once more; taking his seat on the back benches he joined the now strong body of critics (both in and outside the House of Commons) of the Government's prosecution of the war. Later in

---

* George Moore (1852–1933).

† Edward Marsh (1872–1953) was Winston's Private Secretary 1905–8 and 1917–22, and remained a lifelong friend. An art connoisseur and collector, he was a trustee of the Tate Gallery 1937–44. He was created a KCVO in 1937.

5. *Green trees and poppies at Lullenden, 1917–19.* Given by WSC to Sir John
Colville after the war. Collection: Lady Margaret Colville

the summer of 1916 the Dardanelles Commission, ordered by the Prime Minister Mr Asquith, began its hearings. Churchill, eager to have the chance to defend his policies and actions, was a principal witness. But it was not until the following year that an Interim Report of the Dardanelles Commission cleared him of many damaging accusations he had had to bear in silence.

The horrors of the battles of the Somme which had begun in July 1916 dragged on until November; discontent with the Government culminated in Lloyd George's manoeuvring Asquith from power and succeeding him as Prime Minister in December. But Winston faced another eighteen months of frustration before, following on the report of the Dardanelles Commission, Lloyd George (despite Conservative objections) made him Minister of Munitions in July 1917.

Ever since they had given up their 1915 summer's lease of Hoe Farm, Winston and Clementine had yearned for somewhere in the country – 'a little country basket' as they called it. In the spring of 1917 they found what they had been looking for – Lullenden, near East Grinstead: a charming grey-stone house with a small farm. Just the right distance from London for their busy parents, it also made a safe refuge for their children (and Jack and Goonie's brood as well) when the Zeppelin raids started. It was a perfect weekend haven for Winston and Clementine: he found agreeable subjects to paint, and she began to garden with enthusiasm.

The ceasefire at last sounded over the grim lines of trenches in November 1918. Just a few days before the Armistice, Clementine gave birth to their fourth child – a girl whom they named Marigold. In the Khaki Election held in mid-December, the Coalition of Lloyd George's Liberals and Bonar Law's Conservatives swept to power. In this new administration Churchill became Secretary of State for War, and the newly fledged Air Ministry was combined with the War Office under him. He was to hold this office for two years.

Although the whole family loved Lullenden, it soon began to prove a strain on their finances, so less than three years after they had acquired their delightful 'country basket' Winston and Clementine sold the property, deciding for the time being to concentrate their forces in London. They soon found an excellent family house – 2 Sussex Square (now demolished), on the north side of Hyde Park. The mews building at the back was converted into a splendid studio for Winston.

During the spring of 1920, when Clementine was much occupied with moving into their new house, and with the children's school holidays, Winston went off for a highly enjoyable holiday with General Lord Rawlinson, who also loved painting – for his part in watercolours. They were the guests

6. *Sunset at Roehampton, early 1920*. Collection: The Lady Soames, DBE

7. *Self-portrait*, 1919–20. Collection: The National Trust, Chartwell

8. *Sketch of John Lavery's studio*, early 1920s. Collection: The Lady Soames, DBE

9. *Woods at Mimizan, Les Landes,* mid-1920s. Collection: The Rt. Hon. Edward Heath, MBE, MP

of the Duke of Westminster – Bendor, a friend of Winston's since Boer War days – at his house The Woolsack at Mimizan, south of Bordeaux in the Landes. Bendor was prevented by a sudden illness from joining his guests, but Winston and the General made a companionable pair, passing the days in painting and in boar-hunting, for which the region was famous – the Duke had his own pack of hounds. Winston wrote to Clementine on 27 March, soon after their arrival at Mimizan:

> The General and I are entirely alone here and we lead a very simple life divided entirely between riding, painting and eating!
>
> . . . To-night we painted by the lake at a new place, from which we returned by water. The General paints in water colours and does it very well. With all my enormous paraphernalia, I have so far produced very indifferent results here. The trees are very difficult to do and there is great monotony in their foliage; also, water has many traps of its own. How I wish Lavery were here to give me a few hints; it would bring me on like one o'clock. . .[16]

Some years later John Lavery was Winston's fellow guest at Mimizan, and Winston then profited from his advice on how to grapple with the serried ranks of pine trees which are such a feature of the landscape of the Landes. The two painters – the amateur and the professional – painted the same scene from exactly the same viewpoint. Their pictures would later hang side by side at Lochmore Lodge in Sutherland, the Duke of Westminster's home in Scotland, where Winston and Clementine also stayed often, combining painting with salmon-fishing and deer-stalking.

Those ten days in the springtime of 1920 were a true holiday for Winston. He confessed to Clementine:

> I have not done one scrap of work or thought about anything. This is the first time such a thing has happened to me. I am evidently 'growing up' at last. Pouches are however expected today . . .[17]

The contents of the official pouches kept him, as a Minister, informed of political news and events at home. Winston did indeed enjoy a carefree time and found he could relax; yet that spring, as throughout his life, he never willingly let the threads of communication and control slip through his fingers. His self-confessed lapse into idleness was brief; the 'pouches' galvanized him again into action. For the rest of this holiday there was a steady flow of memoranda to the War Office; of letters to the King's Private Secretary, to the King himself (about an appointment), and to divers field marshals and generals on War Office matters.

We have already seen that Winston was far from complacent about his efforts at painting. This springtime of 1920 he completed quite a number of canvases, even settling down to paint after a long day's hunting. That same evening, 31 March, he wrote to Clementine: 'I have painted rather a good picture this evening; the best I have done since coming here – in fact the only one that is tolerable . . .'[18]

In January 1921 Winston and Clementine, heading for the South of France, paused briefly in Paris, where Winston had official business to transact. Before leaving Paris, however, he paid a visit to the Galerie Druet at 20 rue Royale, where the works of a new artist, one Charles Morin, were being exhibited. The Galerie Druet, which existed between 1905 and the mid-1920s, was an important gallery showing the best of the Post-Impressionists as well as figurative artists of the early twentieth century.

Winston was accompanied on his visit to the Galerie Druet by Major Gerald Geiger, the Head of the British Military Mission to Paris, who had been a contemporary of his both at Harrow and at Sandhurst. On 13 January Major Geiger described the official part of Churchill's visit to Paris in a letter to Sir Archibald Sinclair,* at that time Winston's Military Private Secretary, and he added that Winston 'went with me and an art critic to visit the work of the painter CHARLES MORIN. The works of this artist were produced and criticised for forty minutes by the gentlemen in question, and the S of S [Secretary of State] was very interested. . .' Winston surely was 'very interested'[19] – for Charles Morin was his own pseudonym.

According to Professor Thomas Bodkin, Director of the National Gallery of Ireland from 1925 to 1935, writing many years later, six of Winston's pictures shown on this occasion were sold, but he does not mention prices.[20] It must have given great pleasure to Charles Morin to know that at this, the first showing of a number of his pictures, he had a market.

The 'art critic' to whose appraisal Winston lent so attentive an ear would almost certainly have been Charles Montag, whom Churchill had first met in 1915. Charles Montag was born in Winterthur, Switzerland, in 1880, the son of a manufacturer of farinaceous products. He studied art in both Switzerland and Munich, and had his first exhibition there in 1902. Soon the young painter settled in Paris, which became his second home, although he never gave up his Swiss nationality. He made his career chiefly as a landscape painter, and was strongly influenced by the Impressionists, several of whom he knew personally, including Monet, Degas, Pissarro and Renoir. Later he consorted with the next generation of painters – among them

---

* Sir Archibald Sinclair Bt. (1890–1970) was a brother officer with Churchill at Ploegsteert, and close friend thereafter. He was Liberal MP for Caithness and Sutherland 1922–45; Leader of the Parliamentary Liberal Party 1935–45; Secretary of State for Air 1940–45; created first Viscount Thurso of Ulbster 1952.

Bonnard, Vuillard, Manguin, Marquet and Matisse. Montag himself had exhibitions both in Switzerland and Paris, including a one-man exhibition of his work in 1914 at the Galerie Druet. Soon after this he ceased to paint. Through his many contacts he became an organizer of important exhibitions of French art in Switzerland, and an adviser to individual art collectors; he became known as 'l'Ambassadeur de L'Art Français'.

Winston Churchill and Charles Montag met just as the former was taking his first steps in painting, and greatly needed and welcomed the criticism and advice of experts. The two men took a liking to each other, and it was Charles Montag who arranged for his friend to exhibit his paintings for the first time at the Galerie Druet, using the name of Charles Morin. Their friendship was to last until Montag's death in 1956, and over the years Charles would sometimes accompany Winston on painting holidays, escort him round galleries, or write him letters advising him on technical matters such as paints and canvases.

The year following Charles Morin's maiden exhibition, Winston was once again staying at Mimizan. From here he visited Biarritz, accompanied by Eddie Marsh, and wrote to Clementine on 18 August 1922:

> My darling one,
>
> We have only about 50% sunlight tho' perhaps today will turn the scale. Montag has arrived, so our conversation proceeds exclusively in French. I have got several nice pictures under way wh only need an afternoon's sunshine to complete them. Montag is vy anxious to teach me & most austere in all his methods. He was positively glad when the sun didn't shine yesterday because I was forced to give attention to the drawing not having the brilliant light to play with. . .
>
> Tonight we go back to Mimizan, after lunching & painting at St. Jean de Luz – taking Montag with us.[21]

In February 1921 Winston Churchill was appointed Colonial Secretary – a political advancement, for the Colonial Office was then of great importance. Within a short time of assuming his new post Churchill set out on a journey to the Middle East, taking Clementine with him. Their first destination was Cairo, where a conference had been convened to bring about a political settlement in the affairs of Iraq and Transjordan. Prominent among the personalities involved were Colonel Lawrence (Lawrence of Arabia) – with whom the Churchills were soon to become firm friends – and Gertrude Bell, the explorer and Arabist. In this stimulating company Winston and Clementine seized time to visit (and he to paint) the Pyramids (p. 40). The party rode on camels. Not being expert Winston was thrown by his animal and grazed his hand quite badly, but he insisted on remounting

10. *The Pyramids, 1921.* Collection: The National Trust, Chartwell

11. *Jerusalem, 1921.* After the Cairo Conference WSC went on to Jerusalem.
Collection: Winston S. Churchill, MP

and continuing with the others; he then did some painting before camelling back with Colonel Lawrence to the Mena House Hotel, while the rest of the party returned by car. Churchill was not at this time a popular figure with the Egyptians – notices abounded: '*à bas* Churchill!' – but he remained unconcerned. He insisted on setting up his easel in the roadway, and painted away regardless.[22]

The year 1921 saw the climax of the bitter struggle for Irish Home Rule. Great Britain and Ireland signed the treaty in December under which partition (established the previous year) was accepted and Ireland granted Dominion status, thus becoming part of Churchill's direct responsibility as Colonial Secretary. Since the spring of 1920 there had been an upsurge of violence and bloodshed, with dark deeds perpetrated on both sides. It was at this time that Winston's friends John and Hazel Lavery became involved with him in matters more urgent and deadly than brushes and turpentine.

John Lavery was a Belfast-born Roman Catholic and Hazel, although primarily American, had Irish blood in her veins; both had espoused the Nationalist cause, but ardently longed for Britain and Ireland to work out their conflicting ideals and interests by peaceful and constitutional means. After the Great War Lavery had spent much time both in Ulster and in Dublin painting ecclesiastical and political notabilities, and so, with many connections both in Ireland and England, John and Hazel Lavery understood the personalities, passions and problems of the Anglo-Irish drama.

Winston, who always welcomed the unofficial viewpoint, had asked John Lavery to let him know his views on the Irish situation. Churchill, then still Secretary of State for War, was responsible for British troops in Ireland, and as a member too of the Cabinet Committee for Irish Affairs he was deeply involved in all aspects of Ireland and its intractable problems.

It was probably at some time during the winter of 1920, when the partition of Ireland was imminent, that the Laverys, remembering Winston's request, wrote him this moving, and in some ways prophetic, letter:

My dear Minister of War,
   You asked me the other day what I thought of my country's state, and I had not the courage to tell you.
   But if one artist may speak to another I will give you my beliefs.
   The Prime Minister [Lloyd George] has said that he is prepared for a million casualties and a five years' war. I believe that ten million and a fifty years' war would not bring about the result he desires.
   I believe that Ireland will never be governed by Westminster, the Vatican, or Ulster without continuous bloodshed. I also believe that

the removal of the 'Castle'* and all its works, leaving Irishmen to settle their own affairs, is the only solution left.

I am convinced with the knowledge I possess of my countrymen that such a situation would make her one of your staunchest allies instead of an avowed enemy for all time. Love is stronger than hate.

Yours,

Hazel and John[23]

Hazel Lavery especially, with her ardent nature and great social gifts, sought to make links between Englishmen and Irishmen who found themselves increasingly sundered by the bitterness of the issues. Her luncheons and dinners in the house in Cromwell Place saw a vivid mixture of people: 'She had the gift of mixing the Bohemians and the more regulated strata of society. At her table met painter and writer, Cabinet Minister and official, Judge and men who had had a price on their heads.'[24]

As the Treaty negotiations got underway the Laverys did their utmost to bring informally together the Irish negotiators (several of them regarded by the British as blood-stained terrorists), members of the Government, civil servants and others important to the progress of the talks. In particular they fostered the relationship between Winston Churchill and Michael Collins. Now in his early thirties, Collins had taken part in the Easter Rebellion in Dublin in 1916; twice imprisoned by the British, he had been Adjutant-General of the Irish Republican Army, then a Minister in the Sinn Fein Government, and now one of the Irish Delegation. A brave and ardent patriot, he was bent on seeking a peaceful solution to his country's ambitions for self-rule. At first wary of Churchill, he came to trust him; for his part Winston quickly learned to admire Michael Collins's courage, both moral and physical, and his dedication to his country's cause. Later, during the civil war which followed on the signing of the Treaty, Michael Collins commanded the Irish Free State Army against the opponents of the Treaty. In August 1922 he was ambushed and killed by Irishmen: Lavery, a close friend, painted him in death. Churchill had supported him throughout his fatal task of trying faithfully to carry out the provisions of the Treaty, and shortly before his assassination Collins sent a message: 'Tell Winston we could never have done anything without him.'[25]

Hazel Lavery's services to the new Free State of Ireland, and her beauty, were recognized officially when John Lavery was commissioned by the President, William Cosgrave, to paint her portrait, to be reproduced on the first Irish Free State banknotes.

---

* Dublin Castle, the seat of British government in Dublin.

CHAPTER TWO

It was at the end of 1921 that Winston put down on paper his thoughts and feelings about his passion for painting, which had veritably seized hold of him in his middle age: he wrote this 'testament' in the form of two articles for the *Strand Magazine*. Earlier in the year, while considering the proposition, he had discussed it with Clementine. She was not enthusiastic about the project, for she was in principle opposed to Winston's writing what she regarded as 'pot-boilers' to boost their domestic economy. In February 1921 they had been together for a holiday to Nice; Winston then returned to London for his work while Clementine stayed on for a while enjoying the sunshine at St Jean Cap Ferrat, from where she wrote to him on 10 February setting out her reasons for thinking that he should not write the proposed article:

> . . . if you write the Article what are you going to write about
>
> 1) Art in general? I expect the professionals would be vexed & say you do not yet know enough about Art.
>
> 2) Your own pictures in particular? The danger there seems to me that either it may be thought naif or conceited – I am as anxious as you are to snooker that £1000 & as proud as you can be that you have had the offer; but just now I do not think it would be wise to do anything which will cause you to be discussed trivially, as it were . . .[1]

Winston duly considered her point of view, remarking however that

> An article by Mr Balfour on golf or philosophy or by Mr Bonar Law on chess would be considered entirely proper. I think I can make it very light and amusing without in any way offending the professional painters.[2]

Clementine was very often right in her judgements, but with hindsight we must surely be very glad that Winston persevered: the article entitled 'Painting as a Pastime' appeared in two instalments, in consecutive issues

(December 1921 and January 1922) of the *Strand Magazine*. The final version, a small book published in 1948, is pure enchantment to read, throbbing as it does with enthusiasm and encouragement to others to seize brush and canvas and 'have a go', as Winston himself had done several years before, when, under the flail of misfortune, he had discovered in painting a companion with whom he was to walk for the greater part of the long years which remained to him.

Addressing himself to those who like himself discovered painting in middle age, Winston sought to persuade them that

if . . . you are inclined – late in life though it be – to reconnoitre a foreign sphere of limitless extent, then be persuaded that the first quality that is needed is Audacity. There really is no time for the deliberate approach. Two years of drawing-lessons, three years of copying woodcuts, five years of plaster casts – these are for the young. They have enough to bear. And this thorough grounding is for those who, hearing the call in the morning of their days, are able to make painting their paramount lifelong vocation. The truth and beauty of line and form which by the slightest touch or twist of the brush a real artist imparts to every feature of his design must be founded on long, hard persevering apprenticeship and a practice so habitual that it has become instinctive. We must not be too ambitious. We cannot aspire to masterpieces. We may content ourselves with a joy ride in a paint-box. And for this Audacity is the only ticket.[3]

Winston had early in his painting career come to the view that 'oils' were the thing. One of my earliest memories is of my father extolling this medium by chanting the verse:

> *La peinture à l'huile*
> *Est bien difficile,*
> *Mais c'est beaucoup plus beau*
> *Que la peinture à l'eau.*[4]

In *Painting as a Pastime* he goes on to justify his preference:

I write no word in disparagement of water-colours. But there really is nothing like oils. You have a medium at your disposal which offers real power, if you only can find out how to use it. Moreover, it is easier to get a certain distance along the road by its means than by water-colour. First of all, you can correct mistakes much more easily. One sweep of the palette-knife 'lifts' the blood and tears of a morning from the canvas and enables a fresh start to be made; indeed the canvas is all the better for past impressions. Secondly, you can approach your problem from any direction. You need not build downwards awkwardly from white paper to your darkest dark. You may strike where you please, beginning if you will with a moderate central arrangement of middle tones, and then hurling in the extremes when the psychological moment comes. Lastly, the pigment itself is such nice stuff to handle (if it does not retaliate). You can build it on layer after layer if you like. You can keep on experimenting. You can change your plan to meet the exigencies of time or weather. And always remember you can scrape it away.

Just to paint is great fun. The colours are lovely to look at and delicious to squeeze out. Matching them, however crudely, with what you see is fascinating and absolutely absorbing. Try it if you have not done so – before you die.[5]

His enthusiasm is so compelling! No wonder many people have told me how after reading these words they too became convinced that they had to try for themselves. Several, like Winston, have found a lifelong absorption in painting.

Visiting picture galleries had not until this time been a part of Winston's life: nearly forty years later Clementine would tell Lord Moran (Charles Wilson, Winston's doctor from 1941) that

when Winston took up painting in 1915 he had never up to that moment been in a picture gallery. He went with me to the National Gallery, and pausing before the first picture, a very ordinary affair, he appeared absorbed in it. For half an hour he studied its technique minutely. Next day he again visited the gallery, but I took him in this time by the left entrance instead of the right, so that I might at least be sure he would not return to the same picture.[6]

Charles Montag took Winston to the galleries of Paris, and found in him an eager eye. Of this new encounter with art Winston wrote:

Never having taken any interest in pictures till I tried to paint, I had no preconceived opinions. I just felt, for reasons I could not fathom, that I liked some much more than others . . . My friend said that it is not a bad thing to know nothing at all about pictures, but to have a matured mind trained in other things and a new strong interest for painting. The elements are there from which a true taste in art can be formed with time and guidance, and there are no obstacles or imperfect conceptions in the way. I hope this is true. Certainly the last part is true.[7]

12. *Coastal scene near Lympne, Kent*, 1920s. Collection: Mrs Arabella Churchill-MacLeod;
on loan to the National Trust, Chartwell

Under the influence of Charles Montag, who introduced Winston to their work, he fell under the spell of the Impressionists. 'Have not Manet and Monet, Cézanne and Matisse', he wrote,

> rendered to painting something of the same service which Keats and Shelley gave to poetry after the solemn and ceremonious literary perfections of the eighteenth century? They have brought back to the pictorial art a new draught of joie de vivre; and the beauty of their work is instinct with gaiety, and floats in sparkling air.[8]

During the twenties and thirties Winston and Clementine were often the guests of Sir Philip Sassoon,* who with his sister Sybil (married to the fifth Marquess of Cholmondeley) were among their great friends. For two years before his early death in 1939, at the age of fifty-one, Sir Philip was Minister of Works, presiding over the Government art collection and its acquisitions. Among other achievements he was responsible for the restoration to its full glory of Sir James Thornhill's Painted Hall at Greenwich. A great connoisseur of art, he was a Trustee of the National Gallery, the Tate Gallery and the Wallace Collection.

Philip Sassoon was a man of charm, wit and distinction, and he dispensed princely hospitality to a brilliant and varied circle of friends at his two country houses, Port Lympne at Hythe on the Kent coast, and Trent Park, New Barnet, near London. He made a remarkable collection of works of art, many of which passed after his death to his sister, and further embellished the collection of treasures at his brother-in-law Lord Cholmondeley's home, Houghton Hall in Norfolk.

Winston received much help and encouragement from Philip Sassoon, and painted many pictures of both of his houses and gardens. Winston was always fascinated by water and the problems of capturing it, and many of his coastal scenes and seascapes were painted at Lympne. One of the ways in which Winston taught himself to paint was by copying pictures he admired. With his large and varied collection, Sir Philip was able to be of help in this way too, and Winston studied and copied quite a number of his friend's pictures. Sassoon was a friend and patron of John Singer Sargent, and owned many of his works. Winston admired several of these, and found them highly instructive; in 1926 Philip Sassoon wrote Winston this note, which accompanied a generous present and a helpful loan:

---

* Sir Philip Sassoon (1888–1939) succeeded his father both as third Baronet and as Conservative/Unionist MP for Hythe, which he represented from 1912 to 1939. During the First World War he was Private Secretary to Field Marshal Sir Douglas Haig; he was Under-Secretary of State for Air 1924–9 and Minister of Works 1937–9.

13. *Two glasses on a verandah (after Sargent), 1926,* from a picture in the
collection of Sir Philip Sassoon. Collection: The National Trust, Chartwell

13 December 1926

My dear Winston,

You have often admired the picture by John Lewis Brown of the two horsemen that hung at Trent, so I am sending it to you with my best wishes in the hope that you may find a corner for it at Chartwell. I am also sending the little Sargent picture wh you asked for. He painted it when he was 18!

Yours affectionately,
Philip[9]

The 'little Sargent picture' must have afforded Winston many hours of concentrated interest and instruction: the copy he made now hangs at Chartwell (the original is at Houghton). The 'two horsemen' which Philip Sassoon gave Winston, and which he also copied, had an honoured place in his study at Chartwell, where it still hangs.

Another picture from Philip Sassoon's collection which Winston copied was *Ruins of Arras Cathedral*, painted by Sargent when he was on a visit to the war zone in 1918. Winston made two copies of this at different times, and Sargent's influence on his painting of arches and columns can be seen in several of his pictures. It is also possible to trace the lessons he learned from studying Sargent's still life, in his handling of dappled light and leafy shade in pictures such as those he painted of the Palladian bridge at Wilton House, the famous and beautiful home of the Herbert family in Wiltshire. Winston and Clementine stayed here quite often as the guests of the Earl and Countess of Pembroke; indeed their springtime visits, coinciding with Whitsun, were marked in the Wilton visitors' book as 'WINSTONTIDE'. The best of Winston's paintings of the Palladian bridge is now in the private collection of Her Majesty The Queen, to whom he presented it in 1960.

As well as witnessing the deadly struggles over the Irish question on the political front, 1921 had been a year of heavy personal tidings for Winston and Clementine. In June the once beautiful, but still handsome and spirited, Jennie Cornwallis-West (Lady Randolph Churchill), Winston's mother, died in her sixty-eighth year from a haemorrhage after a leg amputation, the result of falling down a staircase. Two months later their beloved child Marigold, aged nearly four, died from septicaemia of the throat.

Battered by grief, Winston and Clementine and their other children took refuge at Loch More in Sutherland, with kind and compassionate Bendor Westminster. Clementine presently had to return to London with the children, whose school holidays were ending; Winston went on to stay with the Duke and Duchess of Sutherland at Dunrobin Castle (on the north-east Scottish coast). From there he wrote to Clementine that he wished she had

14. *The ruins of Arras Cathedral (after Sargent)*, mid-1920s, from a picture in
the collection of Sir Philip Sassoon. Collection: Mrs Arabella Churchill-MacLeod;
on loan to the National Trust, Chartwell

15. *The Palladian Bridge at Wilton,* 1925.
Reproduced by gracious permission of Her Majesty The Queen

16. *Formal garden with statue at Sutton Place, Guildford, Surrey*, early 1920s.
WSC visited the Duke and Duchess of Sutherland and painted at both their homes – in Scotland
and here at Sutton Place – in the 1920s.

17. *Seascape at sunset*, 1920s. Collection: The National Trust, Chartwell

been able to come with him but recognized that the 'enormous party, 25 or 30 mostly extremely young'[10] would hardly have appealed to her at this time. Winston could find distraction and solace in his painting:

> In the afternoon I went out and painted a beautiful river in the afternoon light with crimson and golden hills in the background. I hope to make it much better to-morrow. Geordie [the Duke of Sutherland] wants me to shoot grouse to-morrow. They have a number to be killed, but I think I shall beg off if the weather is fine and go back to my stream.[11]

When sport and painting were competitors for his attention Winston seems to have had no doubt about his choice, for in the same long letter he wrote: 'It is another splendid day: & I am off to the river to catch pictures – much better than salmon.' Winston's letter describing the company and life at Dunrobin was dictated, but the long postscript was handwritten: '. . . Many tender thoughts my darling one of you & yr sweet kittens. Alas I keep on feeling the hurt of the Duckadilly [Marigold's pet name].'[12]

But life and love and hope (fortunately for me) revived, and in

18. *Sunset over the sea: orange and purple*, 1920s. Collection: The Lady Soames, DBE

September 1922 I was born – Winston and Clementine's fifth child. This was also the year that Winston bought Chartwell, near Westerham in Kent: the home he was to love above all others, where he and Clementine and their family were to live for forty years.

At the General Election in November 1922, after the break-up of the Lloyd George Coalition Government, the Conservative Party (having withdrawn from the Coalition) gained a strong majority. Churchill, fighting as a National Liberal, was ousted by the Labour candidate at Dundee, which constituency he had represented for fourteen years. Clementine, although still nursing her six-week-old baby, had to fight the greater part of the electoral campaign for Winston, who had been operated on for appendicitis shortly before, and could only appear in Dundee in the last few days of the battle.

Released from the cares of office, Winston and Clementine swept the whole family off in early December to the sunshine of the Riviera, renting the Villa Rêve d'Or at Cannes for six months. Here Winston recovered his health and strength, worked on the second volume of *The World Crisis*, and also spent many happy sunlit hours painting the colourful scenes around him. For the rest of his life he was to return again and again to this beautiful coast, where the brilliant light and vivid colours appealed greatly to him; he had already, in *Painting as a Pastime*, declared his allegiance to brilliant hues:

> I must say I like bright colours. I agree with Ruskin in his denunciation of that school of painting who 'eat slate-pencil and chalk, and assure everybody that they are nicer and purer than strawberries and plums'. I cannot pretend to feel impartial about the colours. I rejoice with the brilliant ones, and am genuinely sorry for the poor browns. When I get to heaven I mean to spend a considerable portion of my first million years in painting, and so get to the bottom of the subject. But then I shall require a still gayer palette than I get here below. I expect orange and vermilion will be the darkest, dullest colours upon it, and beyond them there will be a whole range of wonderful new colours which will delight the celestial eye.[13]

CHAPTER THREE

Winston must have felt a glow of gratification when in about 1925 he won first prize in an amateur art exhibition held in London at Sunderland House in Curzon Street. The conditions of entry were that the pictures were not to be signed, and that no other indication should be given of their provenance.

Winston sent in what must have been one of his very first pictures of Chartwell; it was probably painted in the winter of 1924/5. Although he had acquired Chartwell in 1922, it was not until two years later, when the considerable alterations, additions and decorations were complete, that the family moved in. The picture, entitled for the exhibition *Winter sunshine* (p. 58), is of the red-brick house painted from the south; pale sunlight shines on melting snow.

The judges of the competition were Sir Joseph Duveen, the great patron of the arts and benefactor of the National Gallery and the Tate; Kenneth Clark, then a young man, but later to be acknowledged as one of the great art historians of our time, a future director of the National Gallery and Surveyor of the King's Pictures; and Oswald Birley, the celebrated portrait painter, who later gave this account of selecting the winning picture:

> . . . Arriving early on the scene, I managed to put on one side all pictures which seemed to have any real merit. I especially noticed a picture of a red house in sunlight with snow on the roof, painted with great vigor – to which I decided, being still alone, to award the first prize.
>
> Later in the morning, Duveen arrived. On showing him my choice of first prize he disagreed firmly, saying, 'No, that is obviously by a professional painter and this is an amateur show.'
>
> I answered that we must assume that its author was an honest man and insisted upon it being given first prize, to which he finally rather grudgingly consented, still apparently certain that it was not by an amateur. Kenneth Clark, who then arrived, upheld my choice and so it was settled.

19. *Winter sunshine, Chartwell, 1924–5*. Collection: Mrs Arabella Churchill-MacLeod

When finally the names of the various prize winners were released by the secretary, we were all delighted and much interested to find that Winter Sunshine had been painted by Winston Churchill.[1]

Twenty-five years later, in 1945, Oswald Birley was commissioned by the House of Commons to paint Winston Churchill, and he and his strikingly beautiful wife Rhoda (who was also an accomplished painter) became great friends of Winston and Clementine. And there was a delightful sequel to the amateur art competition, which will be recorded in its proper place.

Between 1922 and 1924 there were three general elections, in all of which Churchill took part; in addition he fought a by-election in March 1924. In

20. *The Papal Palace at Avignon*, probably 1925. W. H. Orpen, who painted WSC in 1915,
had counselled him to paint at Avignon 'because of the wonderful light'.
Collection: Winston S. Churchill, MP

three out of these four contests he was defeated. During these years he
moved by stages from the Liberal Party (then in total disarray) back to the
Conservative Party, which he had left in 1904 on the issue of Protection.
Churchill was always a Free Trader, and Stanley Baldwin's public abandonment of Protective Tariffs in June 1924 removed the last obstacle to his
reconciliation with the Conservatives. In the General Election in October
1924, newly adopted by the West Essex (Epping) Conservative Association,
Churchill won the seat with a handsome majority; he would represent this
constituency (later renamed Wanstead and Woodford) for forty years. When
Stanley Baldwin formed his second administration in early November,

Winston Churchill was appointed Chancellor of the Exchequer, an office he was to hold until 1929.

In June 1927 Clementine was knocked down by a bus while crossing Brompton Road; happily she was not badly injured, but she suffered from shock and severe bruising. The report of her accident which appeared in the newspapers was read by the painter Walter Richard Sickert, who had known Clementine many years before, at the turn of the century, when as her mother's friend he was a frequent visitor to their house in Dieppe. On an impulse, Sickert marched off to 11 Downing Street and enquired anxiously for news of his friend of so long ago.

Clementine's mother, Lady Blanche, who was separated from her husband, Sir Henry Hozier, had taken her four children to live in Dieppe in the late summer of 1899. A ravishing, eccentric and charming woman, she had soon made many friends, especially among the bohemian and artistic circles of Dieppe society; one of these friends was Walter Sickert, who lived there in the early years of the century. Clementine was fifteen, and she and her sisters Kitty and Nellie went as day pupils to a convent school in Dieppe. Sickert was just forty, clean-shaven, with thick honey-coloured hair and piercing sea-green eyes: Clementine thought he was the most strikingly handsome man she had ever seen, and she was secretly rather in love with him. While doing the shopping for her mother, Clementine would often find Mr Sickert sketching or painting in the charming old squares, or on the street corners of Dieppe. One day, when she had stopped to look at his painting, Sickert asked her, 'Do you like my work?' After rather a long pause Clementine replied, 'Yes.' Noticing her hesitation, Sickert said, 'What is it you don't like?' With characteristic truthfulness Clementine replied, 'Well, Mr Sickert, you seem to see everything with dirty eyes.' Sickert was not the least bit put out by her candour, and subsequently asked her to tea in Neuville-les-Dieppe, the part of the town mostly inhabited by the sea-fishing community, where he had lodgings in the house of Mme Augustine Eugénie Villain, the queen of the Dieppe fishmarket. Famous locally as 'La Belle Rousse', she was Sickert's model and mistress.

A year or two later Clementine was on a sightseeing visit to Paris when Mr Sickert turned up quite unexpectedly and swept her off for a day's gallery visiting, which also included going to see Camille Pissarro in his studio, and having dinner with Jacques-Emile Blanche. During the course of this highly enjoyable day, Clementine asked Mr Sickert, 'Who is the greatest living painter?' To which question Sickert replied quite simply, 'I am, of course.'

Clementine was not to see her eccentric friend until over a quarter of a century later when, full of solicitude for her after her accident, he turned up out of the blue once again. 'I was enchanted to see him after so many years,' she later wrote, "tho his appearance had so much changed that I would hardly have known him – I expect he thought the same of me as I had a black eye and was quite disfigured by my encounter with the bus. He and my husband took to each other immediately . . .'.[2]

It really was a case of 'it's an ill wind that blows nobody any good': Sickert's unheralded reappearance in Clementine's life was to prove of enormous consequence to Winston and his painting, although it was only for a short period of barely two years that he would feature in Winston's life. Sickert and Thérèse Lessore (whom he had married as his third wife in 1926) visited Chartwell, and there were also many painters' colloquies at Number 11. As Clementine recounted, they liked each other, and Sickert was generous with his time and advice to the enthusiastic amateur. The appearance of such a distinguished and brilliant mentor was accidental but perfectly timed: Winston had now been painting for twelve years; he was 'at home' with his brushes, paints and easel; he had tackled a variety of subjects – landscapes, the sea, interiors, still lifes, architecture – and had even ventured into portrait painting. Above all his passion for painting, and his determination to wrestle with the techniques, were unabated, and his eagerness to learn was as keen as ever. Despite the preoccupations and demands of his ministerial life, no opportunity for painting was missed; his paint-box and paraphernalia accompanied him even on the most formal of ministerial visits.

Sickert's advice was conveyed not only during agreeable and stimulating meetings between the two men but also by letter, for he was adept at crystallizing his thoughts and ideas about painting on paper. The evolution of Sickert's own artistic methods can be followed largely through his correspondence with Miss Ethel Sands, an American amateur artist, who had settled in London and held a brilliant salon. During 1913 and 1914 he wrote her 69 letters which are a mine of information and instruction. Now, over ten years later, the great artist was to give a short 'correspondence course' to the Chancellor of the Exchequer of the day.

During the autumn of 1927 Sickert wrote two 'teaching' letters to his new disciple. The letters are concerned with his method of preparing a canvas by creating a '*camaïeu*' (or *camayeu*) – an under-painting of often several layers of paint, composed usually of two colours. The painting instructions are detailed and clear, and interspersed with some delightfully idiosyncratic touches:

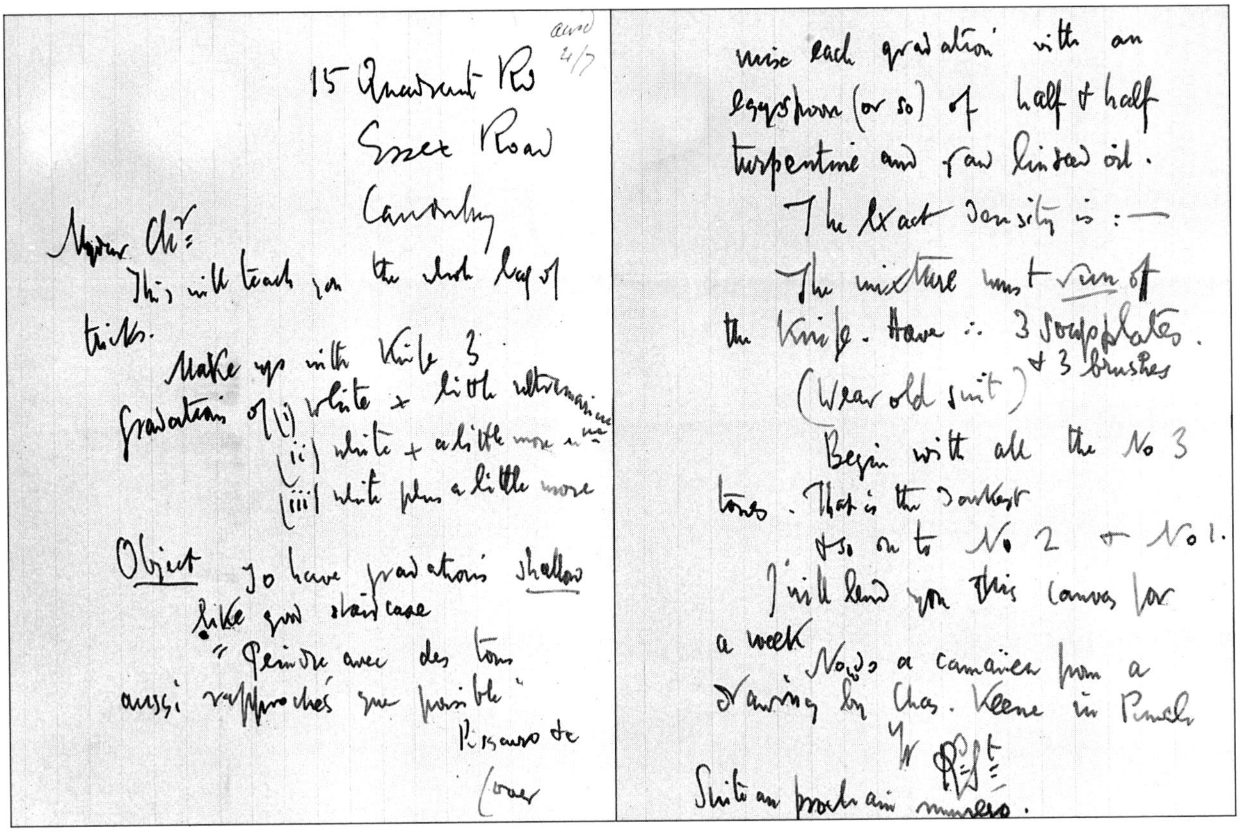

15 Quadrant Rd
Essex Road
Canonbury

My dear Ch[r]

    This will teach you the whole bag of tricks.

    Make up with Knife 3
gradations of   (i) white + a little ultramarine
               (ii) white + a little more u[ne]
               (iii) white plus a little more

Object

    To have gradations <u>shallow</u>
like good staircase
    "Peindre avec des tons
aussi rapprochés que possible"
               Pissarro &c
               (over

mix each gradation with an
eggspoon (or so) of half & half
turpentine and raw linseed oil.
    The exact density is:-
    The mixture must <u>run</u> off
the Knife. Have ∴ 3 soupplates
               & 3 brushes
    (Wear old suit)
    Begin with all the No 3
tones. That is the darkest
    & so on to No 2 and No 1
    I will lend you this canvas for
a week
    Now do a camaïeu from a
drawing by Chas. Keene in Punch

               Y[r]
               R[d] S[t]

Suite au prochain numéro.

Southey Villa
15 Quadrant Rd.
Essex Rd.

My dear Chancellor
    To return to matters of permanent
interest.
    2nd lesson
    Reasons for camaïeu
    Firstly – The old fable of breaking up the
bundle of sticks.   *You can carry on*
half a dozen canvases of camaïeu or
let us say dead-colour with 3 brushes
& three mixtures & not risk polluting your
colour-sense or colour-execution.
    Ideal manner of spreading paint.
    In successive coats with necessary
intervals for drying varying with season &
atmosphere. (Draught drying more than
anything else.) Canvases on high shelves in
incessant draught drying best. (In fact sort of
oast-house)
    Ideal consistency. Colours mixed with
Knife & then diluted with half & half of
oil & turpentine. Raw linseed oil not
bleached. Turps, not refined spirit
of turpentine.
    Until the paint runs
freely off the Knife.
    The white paint is the basis of the quality
of a painting. In England it is called
flake white which of course is not a
definition in law any more than 'nivose'
or 'Schneeweiss' or 'lilywhite' would be. Since
the war you cannot rely on English
flake white, as it is diluted
with zinc white & has no
body. Block x's white is the only good one
now of Terwagne-Clavier, Belgique. L.
Cornelissen of 22 Gt. Queen Street will get it you.
    If each coat is thoroughly dry the
ideal quality is got by a great many
successive coats.

    Now these successive coats. Will
arise normally out of the incessant
corrections & improvements needed in our
progress towards exactness.
    It is only after many coats that
the paint catches so easily, 's'accroche',
as they say in France (hang up like a hat)
that the trace of your brush is an
unhampered record of your mental
intention. This is the main secret of
efficient 'scribble' in oil. You get the
autographic quality which a good quill
gives on highly glazed paper.
    Now you see, if you cannot get a
satisfactory & sensitive autographic freedom
till – say – on the fifth or sixth
coat, why thick paint is not a swaggering
gesture but an inevitable preliminary. It
is what good acoustic conditions are to song.
    Now the disgusting error into
which some who have grasped the fact
that thick paint is a desideratum have
been induced is that, wanting to 'get rich
quick' they put the paint on thick in
one operation. It should get thick by
'de minces couches superposées', thin
coats super imposed at long intervals. Exempli
disgraciae Courbet's use of the palette
Knife to paint with. For why? Because
the paint becomes a bag, shiny without,
and soft within. It never dries properly,
(margin note: the brush leaving the surface after
        each coat minutely currycombed by the bristles
        the Knife leaving it like glass.)
and a shiny surface has no tooth, so
that continued work after one Knife-coat
becomes impossible or, let us say, beastly.
    Relation of dead-colour stage to final picture.
If in your coloured picture we suppose

a hundred gradations in light to dark, your
dead-colour only has three or four, and
those the first three or four say No. 1.
No. 2. No. 3 & No. 4. Therefore in
your final picture there will be ninety-six
more gradations.

Your object, physically, in a
dead-colour is to paint a picture in
white lead. But as that would be
invisible, you get the four lightest
& shallowest gradations possible of
white lead and either red or blue or green or brown.
I left out one most important point
in my first lesson.

Give a coat of the half tone
that is No. 2. to the whole canvas
before you begin, & let that dry.
That serves as a spring-board
(tremplin) from which you paint up
with No. 1. & down with No. 3.

Divide arbitrarily your conception
of your whole picture into light,
half-tone & shadow. It is rather like
transposing a song into the highest
attainable register.

Relation of sketches from nature
to pictures.
Ideal Sketches from nature are like Corot's
early studies of Constable's sketches
practically "once-over", single coats.

Not only are dead-colours necessary preliminaries
to getting the best & freshest result in the end, but
that whole train of thought & practice will
open your mind to a complete understanding
of the nature of painting in colour.
Thank you for your letter
sincerely yours
R^d Sickert*

Sickert also taught Churchill how to make use of photographs, either as preliminary documents for a painting or as *aides-mémoire* to use in the studio to complete a picture. This was not a new development; Sickert had made use of photographs from the earliest days of his painting life and in the last fifteen years used them extensively. The painter who first strongly influenced Sickert was James McNeill Whistler, in whose studio he worked in his early twenties as an assistant; and artists in Whistler's circle made use of photographs for their painting. A little later Sickert was to meet Edgar Degas, whose friendship and influence on him were to endure until his death; Degas too was known to use photographs.[3] In a letter Winston wrote to Sickert on 8 September 1927 he referred directly to this newly taught technique, which he had evidently adopted with enthusiasm, losing no time in equipping himself suitably. The Professor referred to in the letter was Frederick Lindemann, known as 'the Prof'.† Professor of Experimental Philosophy at Oxford, he was Winston's friend and scientific mentor for

---

* It will be observed that these letters are autographed R^d S^t and R^d Sickert respectively; from 1927 he used his second name rather than his first.

† Frederick Alexander Lindemann (1886-1957) was Professor of Experimental Philosophy (Physics), Oxford, 1919-56; Personal Assistant to the Prime Minister 1940-1; created Baron Cherwell 1941; Paymaster-General 1942-5 and 1951-3; Privy Councillor 1943; created Viscount 1956.

nearly forty years. Clementine too was devoted to him, and he was a constant visitor to Chartwell.

8 September 1927

My dear Mr Sickert,

I have been assiduously practising your system. I have executed the preliminary stage of the photograph of St Paul's Cathedral which you sent me, and I have also made another quite successful representation of a Daily Mail photograph.

The Professor insisted on presenting me with a beautiful camera, and I have already taken several photographs which have been developed and enlarged, and which, together with the other sketches, will form the basis of future efforts. I am really enormously obliged to you for your kindness and interest; and when I return to London you must let me have another long consultation with you. When it comes to doing the face on a photograph, or any intricate piece of work, it is quite possible to sub-divide the square or to put criss-cross lines; while the ordinary parts of the picture can be done on the large square.[4]

The last few lines of this letter refer to yet another technique Winston learnt from Walter Sickert – the use of a 'grille or grata ditilo' – a rectilinear grid-like construction which could be expanded or contracted according to the proportional differences in the scale of the preparatory documents and the painted canvas. There is a picture by Winston in the Studio at Chartwell called *Painting lesson from Mr Sickert* (p. 66) which is patently constructed from a photograph; the faint 'grid' lines, made to ensure the right transferred proportions, can be seen, as can Sickert's pencilled directions.

For two days before he wrote to Sickert Churchill had been at Balmoral, and, as was his wont when staying away, he had taken his painting impedimenta with him. No doubt, when the Highland mists allowed, he would have painted the view from his window; but enthralled as he was by the new method to which Sickert had introduced him, he had been working on the photographed view of St Paul's Cathedral mentioned in his letter.

A few weeks later, on 20 September, Winston wrote to Lord Stamfordham, the King's Private Secretary:

I enjoyed myself very much at Balmoral. It is not often that the paths of duty and enjoyment fall so naturally together. I had a particularly pleasant luncheon with the King when we went out deer driving, and a very good talk about all sorts of things. I am very glad that he did not disapprove of my using the Ministerial room as a studio, and I took particular care to leave no spots on the Victorian tartans.[5]

21. *Painting lesson from Mr Sickert, 1927–8.* Sickert's handwritten instructions are visible in the margins. Collection: The National Trust, Chartwell

Before leaving Balmoral, Churchill (at the King's request) presented his painting of *The Cross in St. Paul's Churchyard*,[6] to be auctioned at a local charity sale. The 'auctioneer' was Sir Frederick Ponsonby (Keeper of the Privy Purse) and the picture fetched 115 guineas; Queen Mary presented it to the buyer. On 10 September Sir Frederick wrote to Winston and described the auction:

> In a raucous voice I explained what I was doing. I said that although there were innumerable instances of the King of Scotland giving commissions to famous artists, I defied anyone to find an instance in history of the sovereign of this Country asking a Chancellor of the Exchequer to paint a picture to be sold for charitable purposes . . .[7]

Winston was much diverted and delighted, replying to Lord Stamfordham:

> I was much amused by the cutting which the King sent me. If I could be sure of equally skilful auctioneering, I really might endeavour to reduce our national liabilities by turning out a few pictures. I am so glad that a substantial contribution to the Fund was realised . . .[8]

Back in the south, Winston continued to work at his painting, to which new vistas had been opened. On 20 September he wrote again to Sickert:

> . . . I am deeply interested in all you have shown me, and am most anxious to have a further conclave. Clemmie has been ordered abroad for a rest, and leaves for Venice on Friday. I wonder whether there would be any chance of your coming for the week-end? I would have several camaïeus in various stages of preparation for your inspection, and you could then show me how the colouring stage proceeds. This, you will remember, was only very lightly touched on in our discussion.
>
> The studio will be in working order, and strong, permanent easels and immovable tables will be available instead of the gimcrack structure on which you found me working.
>
> Once more thanking you for so many kindnesses . . .[9]

Clementine left for Venice, as Winston had written, accompanied by Diana (then aged sixteen) for a convalescent holiday. Mr Sickert came to stay at Chartwell as planned and soon after his departure Winston wrote a long letter to Clementine headed '26th September 1927 "Chartwell Bulletin"'. Published weekly – or bi-weekly – it regaled her with all the news from the home front. Of his friend's visit he wrote:

> . . . Sickert arrived on Friday night and we worked very hard at various paintings and had many discussions. I am really thrilled by the field he is

opening to me. I see my way to paint far better pictures than I ever thought possible before. He is really giving me a new lease of life as a painter. . .

In the same letter he considers a plan to join Clementine in Venice:

The Prime Minister returns tonight and I shall probably go to see him tomorrow. I will then find out what his plans are for Cabinets, etc. and will wire you definitely whether I can come or not. I am enormously attracted by the idea of joining you on the Lido and of painting in Venice by my new method. On the other hand every minute of my day here passes delightfully. There are an enormous amount of things I want to do – and there is of course also the expense to consider. Nevertheless I am poising. . .[10]

In another much shorter letter dated the same day, Winston was evidently still pondering the Venetian project:

My darling one,

The sun is shining vy brightly here & the valley might almost in its own way rival yr lagoons. I have not yet heard from Baldwin. Perhaps I will come next week; I will wire you later. But do not expect me or alter in any way yr plans. I hope you will stay fixed in Venice as long as possible & not start 'on tour' as soon as you have sat down. Peace comes from staying in one spot. Write me fully of yr intention, & where you will be next week.

It was always hard for Winston to tear himself away from his beloved Chartwell, but he thought lovingly of his Clemmie, with perhaps a twinge of conscience, for the letter ends:

I have thought vy tenderly about you my Beloved & our life together. You know how much you mean to me, & what I owe you. I will try & be more of a help to you.

Always your loving husband,

W[11]

In the event Winston, accompanied by 'the Prof', set out to join Clementine and Diana in Venice just over a week later, and spent about ten days there with them.

Back in England at the end of October he wrote to Sickert in Paris:

I shall be moving up to London soon and am looking forward to another talk with you. I shall have a few things to show you when we meet.

22. *Tea-time at Chartwell, 29 August 1927,* c. 1928. Clockwise from the front: WSC; Mrs Thérèse Sickert; Hon. Diana Mitford (CSC's cousin, later Lady Mosley); Eddie Marsh; Professor Lindemann; Randolph Churchill; Diana Churchill; CSC; Walter R. Sickert. The empty chair belonged to the photographer, John Fergusson, Private Secretary to successive Chancellors of the Exchequer 1920–38. Collection: The National Trust, Chartwell

23. *The Earl of Balfour, 1928–9.* Lord Balfour, who died in 1930 aged 84,
was a lifelong friend and colleague of both Lord Randolph Churchill and WSC.
Collection: The Marquess of Salisbury

24. *The second Duke of Westminster (Bendor) with his lurcher Sam*, late 1920s.
Collection: Anne, Duchess of Westminster, to whom CSC gave the picture after WSC's death

The Professor came to Venice with me and we experimented on your system with great energy and application. In Paris we bought for £3 10/- a splendid lantern, apparently a trade product, which throws the positive or negative on the canvas exactly the size one wishes. This enables the cameo to be constructed with extraordinary rapidity and accuracy in four or five tints of monochrome. Either you can do it for the negative and paint the whites black and the blacks white, or you can have a lantern slide made and follow the values directly. I have not had a chance yet of trying a portrait by this method but I am sure that a very fair likeness can be produced with great certainty.

We were not quite long enough at Venice to yield the full results. For five days the cameos were being constructed and were drying, and unhappily the sun disappeared at the time when I wished to take these cameos to the actual scene and mark in the colours upon them. You will quite understand this was not intended to be the picture but only the local aide memoire.

I am so sorry to hear you have not been well and trust you have made a complete recovery. All November I shall be in London and I shall propose you an early rendezvous. . .[12]

The 'splendid lantern' was to become part of the resident equipment of Winston's studio; and, as well as sometimes using photographs as 'reminders' of scenes he was painting, he found that by using a magic lantern in conjunction with glass slides projected on to a canvas he could overcome his lack of expertise as a draughtsman, although he would often sketch in the outlines of his subjects with charcoal. Having discovered painting in the middle age of a crowded life, he was loath to spend precious time mastering draughtsmanship, and in the lantern and slides he had found a sensible short-cut which greatly helped him. When he wrote to Sickert in the autumn of 1927 he had not yet tried a portrait by this method, but he was soon to do so, and he achieved quite a number of successful likenesses. Remarkable among them are a head of Lord Balfour (p. 70)* and a charming study of Bendor Westminster, stooping to pat his lurcher (p. 71). Another interesting example is the group he painted of teatime on 29 August 1927 at Chartwell (p. 69): Mr and Mrs Sickert are there, as well as 'the Prof', Eddie Marsh and members of the family. But he never became rigidly tied to photographic methods; he simply employed them as useful aids. My chief memories are of him at his easel, painting directly on to the canvas.

* Arthur James Balfour (1848–1930) was associated in politics with Lord Randolph Churchill as well as with Winston. He became OM and FRS in 1916; the first Earl of Balfour and KG in 1922. He was Prime Minister 1902–5; First Lord of the Admiralty 1915–16; Foreign Secretary 1916–19. His mother was Lady Blanche Cecil, a daughter of the second Marquess of Salisbury.

CHAPTER FOUR

In the General Election in May 1929 the Conservatives failed to win an overall majority, and Ramsay MacDonald formed his second Labour government. Winston Churchill therefore ceased to be Chancellor of the Exchequer, and entered upon a decade out of office; in relation to his career, historians have called these the 'wilderness years'. But one cannot contemplate those ten years, which took Churchill from his middle fifties into his sixty-sixth year, without feeling that though politically he may have been wandering in barren and rocky places, yet there were green oases which blossomed and bore abundant fruit.

Within a few weeks of his resignation Churchill began work on the mammoth undertaking he had been contemplating for some little while: the writing of the history of his great ancestor John, Duke of Marlborough. The four volumes of this work, considered by some to be his masterpiece, appeared between 1933 and 1938. But before the publication of the first volume Churchill had already written and published *The Aftermath* in 1929; *My Early Life* in 1930; *Thoughts and Adventures* and *The Unknown War* in 1931. From 1937 he was beginning to work on his panoramic four-volume *History of the English-Speaking Peoples*, and for some months work on this formidable project ran in tandem with writing and correcting the last of the *Marlborough* volumes.

The writing, correcting and revising of these books represented a continuous programme of concentrated work, in which he was helped by a team of brilliant historical assistants and devoted secretaries, who in relay, and usually after dark, took his dictation for hours on end. I have listed the major works achieved in that decade, but alongside these there was also an astonishing tally of articles for newspapers and magazines.

Then of course there were also the political speeches, over which Churchill toiled with passionate care; 'Be quiet: your father is with speech' was a frequent injunction from my mother. Politics always came first – there lay Winston Churchill's destiny – and all his other work and pleasures were subordinated to the times and seasons of Parliament and the uncertain but overriding commands of political events. Yet he found time – or made it – to enjoy himself; to be brilliant and convivial company; to reorganize the landscape at Chartwell; to build (with his own hands) walls and cottages; and to paint. Much earlier (in 1922) Lord Robert Cecil, a parliamentary friend,* had poked fun at Winston's many-sided activities, and sharpened his political stiletto too, as he parodied Dryden at his friend's expense:

> Stiff in opinion, always in the wrong,
> Was everything by starts and nothing long,
> But in the course of one revolving moon,
> Was scribbler, painter, statesman and buffoon.[1]

Recalled after over half a century the jibes have lost their sting and acquired an element of irony.

From a painting point of view, too, the thirties were years of prodigious output for Winston. At a rough estimate, of the 500-odd canvases which are now extant, 250 were painted between 1930 and 1939, a period when arguably Winston reached the peak of his powers as a painter. This judgement is reflected in the choice of his pictures illustrated here.

Released from high office in the early summer of 1929, Winston made plans for a journey to Canada and North America which would combine various strands of interest, business and enjoyment. He had not visited the great continent since 1900, and he had never 'been West'. He planned to lecture, promote his newly published *The Aftermath*, and collect material for newspaper articles; he assured William Randolph Hearst (the newspaper proprietor), 'I have no political mission and no axe to grind.' His companions were his son Randolph, aged eighteen, his brother Jack, and his nephew Johnnie Spencer-Churchill. Clementine, to her disappointment, was kept at home by ill health – she had suffered a mastoid operation in 1928, and been laid low in July 1929 by another operation, this time for tonsils.

The party set out in the first week of August in the *Empress of Australia*, disembarking at Quebec. The Churchills then boarded the train to which their own private railway car (the *Mount Royal*, loaned by a Canadian steel magnate) was attached. This wonderful amenity, with its creature comforts and observation car, made their journey most agreeable. Their 'trail' included Montreal, Ottawa, Toronto and Winnipeg; then the prairies gave way to the oilfields, and they visited Calgary and Edmonton. Winston was thrilled by the buoyancy of this great country and its people, and he regaled

---

* Later, as Viscount Chelwood, he would be President of the League of Nations and, in 1937, winner of the Nobel Peace Prize.

Clementine at home with vivid descriptions of all that his observant eye saw, the beauties and wonders of the scenes along their route.

The Churchills left the train at Calgary and drove eighty miles to Banff. By 27 August they had arrived at Banff Springs Hotel, where they paused for breath. Winston described the pace of the last three weeks in a letter to Clementine dated 27 August 1929:

> We have never ceased travelling, starting, stopping, packing, un-packing, scarcely ever two nights in any one bed except the train; & eight nights running in that. Racket of trains, racket of motor, racket of people, racket of speeches! I have made 9 & have 2 more. It has been a whirl: & on arriving here last night after the motor drives of 80 miles with a long speech at Calgary between them, I decreed a halt. So we stay here 36 hours in this magnificent hotel with every comfort – an out-door swimming pool kept at 90° & riding – & I am going for the first time to try & paint a picture. I went to bed at 10 utterly tired out: & have just wakened at 7.30![2]

This tour had not been planned as a painting holiday, but of course Winston had brought his paints with him 'in case', and the three-day trip through the Rocky Mountains that he and his party now embarked on provided him with ample subjects. On the second night he painted at Lake Emerald, which he described as 'an extraordinary colour more turquoise or Jade than Emerald'.[3] They stayed at the nearby Bungalow Camp belonging to the Canadian Pacific Railway, and he told Clementine that 'I painted three pictures which give a very inadequate idea of the great beauty of this spot.'[4] The last day of their mountain holiday was spent visiting Lake Louise, where Winston painted green waters vivid against a backdrop of granite walls and snowy peaks.* Then, once more in the train, they headed through the Fraser valley to Vancouver, where their Canadian tour ended.

The American leg of their journey took Winston and his family party from west to east. They visited Seattle and San Francisco, and went to see William Randolph Hearst at San Simeon; they met film stars (including Charlie Chaplin) and fished for swordfish in Los Angeles; they took a brief glimpse at the yawning void of the Grand Canyon; they paused in Chicago; and on 18 October reached New York City. By this time Winston was travelling alone, for Randolph and Johnnie had left for home and the term at Oxford a week or two before. Winston was in New York for the Great Crash of the American stock markets in the last week of October, in which he himself lost what was to him a small fortune. Fortunately, during his

---

* Three pictures from the Canadian tour are in the Studio at Chartwell.

journey in the United States, he had signed several highly lucrative contracts for articles in weekly magazines; his pen and his unfailing industry would keep the wolf from the door, but this sudden loss of a major capital sum was a severe blow, and cast a shadow over his otherwise joyful return home to Clementine and Chartwell.

The 1929 Wall Street Crash, in which Winston received a mauling, ushered in a period of three years when financially, politically, and in his health he would be in the doldrums. As a result of his financial losses the Churchills' home economy was subjected to a reign of stringency – the rigours of which varied in degree from time to time. While Winston had been Chancellor of the Exchequer they had lived at 11 Downing Street; now, instead of buying a London house, they either rented furnished houses for short periods, or stayed in a hotel. The style and scale of life at Chartwell was much reduced, and my parents, my governess and I spent one winter very cosily in a newly finished, charming small house on the property; Winston had done much of the brickwork himself. Originally intended to house a married butler, it now came in most opportunely as our 'slump' retreat.* Winston's study in the 'big' house was kept open so that he and his secretary and researchers could work, and the Studio in the garden was a sacrosanct haven. One area where the hand of economy was most noticeable was in travels abroad purely for pleasure or painting; indeed none are recorded for some time now.

In the political field Winston found himself so strongly at odds with his party's policy on India that in January 1931 he resigned from Baldwin's Business Committee (Shadow Cabinet in modern parlance), of which he had been a member since the defeat of the Conservative Government. This had the consequence that when seven months later, as a result of the severe economic crisis in Britain, Ramsay MacDonald invited members of the Conservative and Liberal parties to form a National Government, Churchill was not one of the Conservatives included; nor would he be after the General Election which shortly followed, when the National Government was returned with a handsome majority. He was now truly in political limbo.

With no ministerial obligations, Winston undertook a lecture tour in America, with the chief purpose of recouping some of the losses he had suffered two years before, and he left England in early December 1931, taking Clementine and Diana with him as companions to cheer him along during the arduous weeks of the tour programme. Within two days of his arrival in New York disaster struck: crossing Fifth Avenue on the evening of 13

---

* Named 'Wellstreet', it is now the home of the National Trust Administrator at Chartwell.

December, on his way to visit his great friend, the financier and statesman Bernard Baruch, Winston was knocked down by a car travelling at some speed. Fortunately he was wearing a heavy, fur-lined coat, otherwise the results of the accident would certainly have been more severe. As it was he sustained a severe scalp wound, two broken ribs and heavy bruising, and subsequently developed pleurisy. When Winston was released from hospital he returned in a weak state to the Waldorf-Astoria, where he, Clementine and Diana spent a quiet Christmas. For the New Year they all went to Nassau in the Bahamas, where they remained for the first three weeks of January 1932. Winston had been severely knocked about, and his recovery in both health and spirits was slow. These holiday weeks were ones of continuing weakness, low spirits, and anxiety as to the speed and extent of his recovery.

Clementine too was anxious, and wrote to Randolph on 12 January:

> Papa is progressing but very very slowly. I am sure he will be again as well as before, but he is terribly depressed at the slowness of his recovery . . . Last night he was very sad and said that he had now in the last 2 years had 3 very heavy blows. First the loss of all that money in the crash, then the loss of his political position in the Conservative Party and now this terrible physical injury. He said he did not think he would ever recover completely from the three events . . . I had hoped he would paint here but he does not seem to have the strength or energy to start. He bathes every morning and likes that but he stays in only a few minutes in the shallows. . .[5]

Just over a week later Winston reported that he had made a decided improvement,[6] but in this crisis in his life his friend the Muse of Painting had not been able to come to his rescue. He wrote to Randolph: 'I have not felt like opening the paint box, although the seas around these islands are luminous with the most lovely tints of blue and green and purple. . .'[7]

Churchill's God-given strong constitution, and his own determination not to default on his lectures, combined to enable him to resume his tour at the end of January, and in the next month he spoke in twenty different cities to enthusiastic audiences. Winston, Clementine and Diana arrived home in England on 17 March, and went straight to Chartwell, where he lay low for about a month, thoroughly recovering his health and strength. He was not idle during these weeks, however, for he busied himself with his Marlborough papers.

By 30 April Winston had recovered both bounce and *bonhomie*, as his speech at the Royal Academy Dinner demonstrated; in it he teased both the Prime Minister, Ramsay MacDonald, and Stanley Baldwin (Lord Privy Seal and Lord President of the Council) in terms enjoyed by his hosts and his audience alike. We have only his notes for the speech, but they make diverting reading. Of the Prime Minister he said:

> His works are well-known;
>> regret not more of them at home . . .

> I have watched many years
>> his style and methods.

> For long time
>> thought too much vermillion
>>> in his pictures

> Those lurid sunsets of Empire,
>> and capitalist civilisations,
>>> began to pall on me.

> Very glad altered his style so fundamentally.

> In all his new pictures
>> see use of cobalt, French ultramarine,
>>> Prussian blue,
>>>> and all other blues,
>>>>> especially cerulean – a heavenly colour.

> Uses blue now like Sargent,
>> not only for atmosphere,
>>> but even as foundation.

> I like his modern style much better
>> than his earlier method.

Churchill went on to speak about Baldwin:

> If criticised –
>> little lacking in colour,
>>> and in precise definition
>>>> of objects in foreground.

> He too has changed in later life
>> not only his style but his subjects.

> We all miss very much
>> those jolly old-English scenes
>>> he used to paint.

The Worcestershire farm,
    Pigs in clover,
        brocolli in Autumn,

and above all, just now,
    'Brewing the audit ale'.

Still must admit
    something very reposeful
        his twilight studies
           in half-tone. . .

And about himself:

But sure you will ask
    why I am not exhibiting this year,
        why no important pictures on the line?

Frankly, differences with the Committee
    and this year
        not submitting any of my works
           for their approval.

Joined the teaching profession –
    a sort of Slade school.

We have a very fine lot of young students,
    and glad to assist them
        in learning some rudiments
           of parliamentary technique.

Still a few things on easel
    which I hope some day
        present to public.[8]

Winston was much touched a few days later to receive a charming letter from Mr Baldwin which showed he had taken Churchill's jocularity in good part. Indeed he responded in like style:

My dear Winston,
    I am profoundly touched by your generous appreciation of my work as expressed in your speech at the Academy on Saturday night.
    There is so much jealousy in the art world that a kind word to the painter from so distinguished an exponent of a far different style shews a breadth of mind as [words missing] it is delightful.
    And I am glad to think that although my own preference is for still

25. *The North Porch, the Manor House, Cranborne, Dorset, 1932.* Given by WSC to Viscount Cranborne (Bobbety), later fifth Marquess of Salisbury. Collection: Viscount Cranborne

life and half-tone, I do enjoy the bright and sometimes fierce lights in which you revel, and no one will be more interested than I when you come to exhibit the work which is still on your easel.

Yours always

S.B.[9]

Churchill, in thanking Mr Baldwin, wrote: 'I was vy glad my chaff did not vex you. My shafts though necessarily pointed are never intentionally poisoned . . .'[10]

But his run of bad luck was not finished yet. In pursuit of his labours on the life of the Great Duke, Winston decided to do some personal research; accordingly, towards the end of August, a congenial caravan set out to tour the most important of his ancestor's fields of victory. The party consisted of himself, Clementine and Sarah, 'the Prof', and Lt-Col. Pakenham-Walsh, the military historian. In Belgium they visited the battlefields of Ramilles, Oudenarde and Malplaquet; then they set out on the long drive (but how much longer a march for Marlborough's army) to Blenheim, in Bavaria. Afterwards the family planned to go on to Venice, but while they were still in Bavaria Winston was laid low with fever, soon diagnosed as paratyphoid. He was in a Salzburg sanatorium for two weeks, returning towards the end of September to Chartwell. He was still not fully recovered, but set to work on his chapters to make up for lost time, working mostly in bed. He got up too soon, collapsed with a haemorrhage and a recurrence of paratyphoid, and was whisked to a London nursing home by ambulance, in quite a serious state.

In October at Chartwell he was able to resume his work, while recovering from his relapse. His secretary, Mrs Pearman, wrote to a colleague on 20 October: 'Mr Churchill is steadily improving, though progress is rather slow, but as usual nothing can keep him from work. . .'[11] A severe chill in December laid him low again for a short spell, finally ending the tally of illnesses which had dogged him now for over a year.

In November 1932 Winston celebrated his fifty-eighth birthday. His workload that winter consisted not only of *Marlborough*, the *English-Speaking Peoples* and *Great Contemporaries*, but also included many newspaper and magazine articles. This formidable programme also kept his team of research assistants, historical advisers and secretaries constantly on the go.

CHAPTER FIVE

In the thirties Winston much enjoyed the company and counsel of the well-known French painter Paul Maze. They had first met in 1916, but it was not until the thirties that the two men saw each other a good deal. In 1934, Paul Maze wrote to Churchill asking him to write the introduction to his war memoirs, *A Frenchman in Khaki*. Winston was pleased to do this, for he had always admired Maze's gallantry, which was recognized both by his own compatriots and by the British; he had been awarded the Distinguished Conduct Medal, the Military Medal and Bar, the Légion d'Honneur, and the Croix de Guerre.

Born of French parents, Maze was educated both in France and in England. Aged twenty-seven when the war broke out, he was a conscript soldier, whose health and physique could have excused him from the duty of military service; despite this, he managed to be constantly within the reach of shells and bullets. He became, through his perfect knowledge of English and French, and his urgent desire to be in the thick of it all, an unofficial liaison officer with the Royal Scots Greys. Although he was only a sergeant (*sous-officier*) he gained the confidence of their commanding officer, and later that of two successive commanders in the British Expeditionary Force, Generals Gough and Rawlinson.

One of the tales my father used to delight in recounting about Paul Maze was how, while attached to the Royal Scots Greys, in the confusion of the retreat from Mons at the end of August 1914, he became separated from his unit and fell under deep suspicion of being a spy. He was actually being led out to summary execution by a firing party on the orders of a British general when, in the nick of time, the Royal Scots Greys came clattering down the village street, and one of their officers recognized their interpreter.

Paul Maze married Margaret Nelson,* the widow of one of his friends killed in action, and for the most part made his home in Britain, where his

* This marriage was dissolved in 1949: in 1950 he married Jessie Lawrie.

painting came to be admired. One of his principal patrons was Lord Ivor Spencer-Churchill (second son of the ninth Duke of Marlborough, and a cousin of Winston); he was also a friend of Earl De La Warr and his wife, who owned many of his paintings and were country friends and neighbours of the Churchills. So there were several links which brought Maze and Churchill naturally together.

Winston valued Paul's advice on painting and found his ebullient company most congenial. Paul's interests and views were not confined to the arts; a strong Anglophile, he saw Churchill as the great champion of Anglo-French co-operation. As the thirties advanced, Maze understood the dangers that loomed ahead, and was an ardent supporter of Churchill's lonely fight to awaken Britain and France to the menace of Hitler's growing power. On 9 March 1936, Hitler's forces occupied the Rhineland; Churchill urged joint action by France and Britain, calling on the League of Nations to support France and give her justice and satisfaction. He expressed his views in an article in the *Evening Standard* on 13 March (one of a series on current affairs), and that same day Paul Maze wrote to him:

> My dear Winston,
>
> This is just to tell you that you are much in my thoughts during this crisis.
>
> How right you have been as events alas now prove. The public is slowly beginning to see it. I am hoping that a strong line will be taken. Hitler will come to heel if he knows that all the countries are against him as they surely will be. As you say in the Evening Standard 'it is a wonderful chance we are now offered & we must take it'. *Do* write to all the papers you can – the German propaganda spread about is most harmful especially in Mayfair society.
>
> Keep well – England needs you now more than ever, and I only hope that the Government will have the sense of putting you at the helm of defence.
>
> Yours ever,
> Paul[1]

Over a year later, on 12 November, Paul Maze attended the Defence Debate in the House of Commons, and heard Churchill's moving of an amendment in which he stated that Britain's defences were 'no longer adequate' for the safety and freedom of the British people. In a telling sentence he reproached the Government:

> So they go on in strange paradox, decided only to be undecided, resolved to be irresolute, adamant for drift, solid for fluidity, all

powerful to be impotent. So we go on preparing more months and years – precious, perhaps vital, to the greatness of Britain – for the locusts to eat.[2]

Afterwards Paul wrote to Winston, combining political appreciation with some practical advice on painting:

My dear Winston,

I was thrilled by every word you said in the House yesterday – as I went down, the usher downstairs said to me 'you chose a good day to come, he is always fine – none left like him – he always does one good'.

I nearly embraced him – I feel so much what he said! I have sent you some brushes – you should destroy most of your old brushes which can't help you in your work. Paint like you write or speak. You can do it – every stroke of the brush must be a statement felt & seen – Remember that '*En peinture il faut que a tout moment le tableau soit beau – il ne faut jamais mettre quelques touches qui ne le sert pas – il est toujours plus facile de pousser une toile loin quand on est parti de la vérité*' . . .[3]

The trace of 'buccaneer' spirit in Paul Maze was one of the characteristics which attracted Winston to him. The same was true of others among Winston's closest friends, such as F. E. Smith (first Earl of Birkenhead), Max Beaverbrook and Brendan Bracken, and it may have been this same 'buccaneer' element which Clementine instinctively disliked in all of them. Paul Maze visited Chartwell many times (although, curiously, he only signed the Visitors' Book once), but after a while Clementine found his recurrent presence tiresome, and the visits ceased. Winston and he kept in touch, and all met with cordiality at Blenheim, and at St Georges-Motel near Dreux, the home of Consuelo Balsan (mother of Ivor Spencer-Churchill), where Winston and Clementine were often visitors, and where the Maze family frequently stayed at the Moulin de Montreuil in the grounds of the château. But Maze never became at Chartwell a universally enjoyed friend and companion in the way that William Nicholson did.

William Nicholson first came into Winston and Clementine's life in the summer of 1934, when this brilliant painter, and a man of enormous and idiosyncratic charm, came to Chartwell to paint a conversation piece, commissioned by a group of the Churchills' friends to mark their Silver Wedding (celebrated the previous year). Many years later Winston was to tell Sir John Rothenstein, then Director of the Tate Gallery: 'I think the person who taught me most about painting was William Nicholson . . .'[4]

By this time Nicholson was a highly esteemed artist, and particularly in demand as a portrait painter. As a young man, he and his brother-in-law

James Pryde had revolutionized poster art under the name of the 'Beggarstaff Brothers'; some of their designs are now in the Victoria & Albert Museum. Nicholson then moved on to woodcuts, and Heinemann published his now famous *Alphabet* and other illustrated books. The world of the theatre held a fascination for him, and he went on to design the first production of *Peter Pan* in 1904; much later he was to do the sets for Massine's ballets in *On with the Dance* in 1925. As he matured he began to paint landscapes, still lifes and finally portraits. As the early influences faded, his style gradually changed, and the boldness of his early work 'gave way to an exquisite refinement of subdued tone, pale, clear colour, and firm confident handling of paint for which it would be hard to find a parallel in English painting'.[5]

Nicholson soon became a favourite with the whole Churchill family; sittings for the picture were a pleasure, not a tribulation. After these William would take himself off to paint elsewhere; he painted some lovely pictures (which, alas and alack, my mother was to sell in the last years of her life) of Chartwell scenes – notably of the black swans. When he wasn't painting, or talking to Winston about painting, he would often come to my schoolroom (in 1934 I was twelve) to play a lovely game he had invented: he would fill a piece of paper with oval to round shapes – tier upon tier of them – to represent a football crowd, and then we would all take turns at filling in the features and expressions. He would also draw my pug-dog; and he never tired of sketching our beautifully marked marmalade cat. The charcoal drawings he made of my large family of ill-assorted dolls are precious possessions to me now. In *Who's Who* Nicholson named his recreations as 'boomerang, *bilboquet*'; going for walks with him was made both fascinating and frightening by his very nicely judged throwing of the boomerang; while it was a quieter, indoor diversion to watch (and try unsuccessfully to emulate) his skill and diversity with the *bilboquet*, or cup-and-ball. All these talents were appreciated by grown-ups and children alike.

William was a considerable dandy, and he dressed with meticulous and unconventional fastidiousness: he wore extremely elegant, delicately spotted shirts and canary-coloured waistcoats. His charm, like all else about him, was subtle, and his friendship 'for all its warmth and generosity, was neither intimate nor hearty'.[6] Despite his own quiet variety of charm, William seemed to tolerate our family's occasional uproariousness. Clementine soon became devoted to 'S'William', as we called him after he was knighted in 1936 (an accolade he accepted, although he refused election to the Royal Academy). Between 1934 and the war, 'S'William' – or, as Winston preferred to call him, 'Cher Maître' – was a regular visitor to Chartwell.

Clementine greatly welcomed the influence he had, by example and precept, on Winston's palette and style of painting. Loving the brilliant colours as he did, Winston tended sometimes towards the too bright or too hard; he himself (at times reluctantly) recognized this. Quite soon after Nicholson first appeared upon the scene, Clementine, writing to Winston in the South of France, enjoined him: 'I love to think of you painting sparkling sun-lit scenes – Are you keeping them cool & pale à la Nicholson?'[7] A few days later Winston replied: 'I have painted four pictures and begun another. I think the Notre Dame de Vie, à la Nicholson – vy luminous. It is the best I think I have yet done. . .'[8]

Nicholson's painting of Winston and Clementine, the initial cause of this delightful and fruitful friendship, hung in the dining room at Chartwell where it was painted. The 'Cher Maître' took artistic licence in depicting my parents at breakfast together: it was a meal they rarely shared throughout the course of their 57 years of marriage! But it was a delightful picture, and the artist caught my parents' attitudes and likenesses. For me, it also evoked all the charm of that dining room on a sunny day, with the door open into the garden, one of my only too numerous bantams strolling in on the look-out for crumbs, and Tango, the adored cat, sitting on the newspapers on the table. But a curious and rather tragic circumstance surrounded this picture. In 1942 there was a retrospective exhibition of Nicholson's work at the National Gallery, and he asked to borrow the picture of my parents for it. William, then seventy, took against the painting on seeing it again and started to repaint it, but failing to get it right he destroyed it. Marguerite Steen, who was William's great friend and companion, came to see Clementine soon after the war to tell her the sad story. In her book *Pier Glass: More Autobiography* Miss Steen wrote that 'No one could have been kinder than Mrs Churchill, when I went to see her at Hyde Park Gate and broke to her the news of the disaster. . .'[9] Fortunately the highly advanced sketch for the picture survived, and this still hangs in the dining room at Chartwell today.*

---

* There is also a small version of the picture, now on loan to Churchill College, Cambridge, from the Methuen Estate Settlement Trust.

CHAPTER SIX

Winston's long love-affair with the Riviera had really started in that winter of 1922 when, as he had put it himself, he was 'without an office, without a seat, without a party, and without an appendix'.[1] The Churchills had then taken a villa in Cannes for six winter months, during which he wrote and painted away to his heart's content. Clementine too was enjoyably occupied: she had a new baby (me) and an agreeable house; and she was at the peak of her tennis-playing. But during the remaining years of the twenties there were not many opportunities to revisit the sunlit scenes which had so beguiled Winston, for by the autumn of 1924 he was back in Stanley Baldwin's second government as Chancellor of the Exchequer, an office which he retained until the Government's defeat in 1929. He did manage to fit in some agreeable holidays, nevertheless; in particular two excursions to Italy – one to Florence in 1925, and another to Venice in October 1927.

Among Winston and Clementine's close mutual friends were Consuelo and Jacques Balsan; Consuelo, born a Vanderbilt, was Winston's cousin by her marriage to the ninth Duke of Marlborough. That marriage was surely one of the unhappiest examples of an 'arranged match' – or mismatch – and after eleven years of reigning as Duchess at Blenheim Palace, and bearing two sons, Consuelo had left her husband. She was a solitary but dignified figure for many years, then in 1921 she married a charming Frenchman, Jacques Balsan, with whom she was to be supremely happy for the rest of their long lives. Soon after their marriage, the Balsans had established themselves on a clifftop above Eze-sur-mer, in a beautiful domain – Lou Sueil. Here they often invited the Churchills; Clementine liked to make a yearly visit in February and Winston would sometimes join her there. Later the Balsans acquired a most lovely sixteenth-century château, St Georges-Motel, near Dreux, about fifty miles north of Paris. Here too the Churchills were most hospitably invited, and they would often visit there in the late summer months. In her memoirs Consuelo Balsan gives a charming account of Winston, the artist, setting forth on a painting expedition:

He used to spend his mornings dictating to his secretary and his afternoons painting either in our garden or in some other site that pleased him. His departure on these expeditions was invariably accompanied by a general upheaval of the household. The painting paraphernalia with its easel, parasol and stool had to be assembled; the brushes, freshly cleaned, to be found; the canvases chosen, the right hat sorted out, the cigar box replenished. At last, driven by our chauffeur, accompanied by a detective the British Government insisted upon providing, he would depart with the genial wave and rubicund smile we have learned to associate with his robust optimism. On his return he would amuse us by repeating the comments of those self-sufficient critics who congregate round easels. An old Frenchman one day told him, 'With a few more lessons you will become quite good!' – a verdict connoisseurs have already endorsed.[2]

During the thirties, despite his enormous literary output and his total involvement in politics, Winston generally enjoyed uninterrupted holidays, and it was during these years that he regularly sought the sunshine scenes of the South of France which so beguiled him. During these years his most frequent port of call was the Château de l'Horizon at Golfe-Juan, near Cannes, the home of Miss Maxine Elliott. In 1933, the year Winston and Clementine first went to stay with her in her recently completed house, Maxine Elliott was about sixty-five, and a figure from the high Edwardian past.

She had been born Jessie Dermot[3] in 1868, in Rockland, Maine, the daughter of an Irish immigrant sea-captain. When she was only sixteen she married a New York lawyer, George MacDermott, but he was both drunken and quarrelsome, and within four years she left him. Determined to be independent, Jessie decided upon a stage career, and after initial discouragements – being beautiful, lively and talented – she made her way up the theatrical ladder, changing her name *en route* to Maxine Elliott. She became increasingly successful, and toured the United States with well-known companies. In 1896 Maxine married a man twelve years her senior: Nat C. Goodwin, a celebrated comedian and actor-manager. For the next seven years or so theirs was a remarkable partnership, in which he relied greatly on her judgement and keen financial acumen.

The Goodwins came regularly to England, where their plays became a feature of the London season. Maxine's success in England was dazzling; her forte was light romantic comedy, and with her beauty and the sumptuous clothes she always wore, she made her name and fame.

Soon doors in London society opened to her, largely through the Keppels, who took a great liking to her. Mrs Keppel held the key to the

26. *Coastal scene near Cannes*, mid-1930s. Collection: The Lady Soames, DBE

27. *The harbour at Cannes*, 1930s. Collection: The Lady Soames, DBE

28. *A church in the South of France*, mid-1930s. Collection: The Lady Soames, DBE

golden inner circle of London society through her long friendship with the Prince of Wales, now King Edward VII. Alice Keppel took Maxine up and introduced her to her friends, including the King. At thirty-three, little Jessie Dermot had indeed come a long way from Rockland, Maine: her beauty and elegance, lively wit and strong personality, combined with perfect manners and *savoir faire*, made her a welcome newcomer to Edwardian society. Clever and powerful men liked her: both Lord Rosebery and Lord Curzon at various times proposed marriage to her, but she turned them both down. Riches and position appealed to her, but above all Maxine Elliott valued her own independence.

During these years the Goodwins had drifted apart, and in 1905 they were divorced. But Maxine was now a rich woman in her own right, through unremitting hard work and shrewd management of her financial affairs. A few years later she opened her own theatre in New York, and in 1910 she bought Hartsbourne Manor at Bushey Heath in Hertfordshire, an hour's journey from London, where she entertained in memorable style.

The Hartsbourne parties soon became famous for their stimulating mixture of personalities from the worlds of politics, business, *haute finance* and social life. Maxine was a snob, and dearly loved a lord, but she also enjoyed the company of achievers – of which she was herself such a signal example. Sometime around 1906 Winston and Maxine had met, and after his marriage he and Clementine were made welcome at Hartsbourne.

The outbreak of war in 1914 put an end, along with much else, to that glittering and agreeable life of which Hartsbourne was a part. Although she was an American born and bred, Maxine identified herself completely with the Allies' cause from the beginning. Struck by the misery of the Belgian peasant population caught between the great contending armies, Maxine bought, equipped and organized a relief barge entirely from her own resources: in fifteen months she fed and clothed some 350,000 refugees.

After the war she returned to the stage in America and rebuilt her fortune, even making a brief sortie into the world of film-making – but the cinema was not really her medium. Being a realist she recognized that, at forty-eight, her professional days were fading, and in 1920 she retired finally from the stage. Returning to England she opened up Hartsbourne again, but the 'great days', and many of those who had made them, were gone for ever. Although her friends still came (one of the early photographs of Winston painting was taken there), the spirit and style of the place had faded, and in 1923 she sold Hartsbourne. Soon she moved to Paris; and for the next few years the vacuum left by her professional career and the abandonment of her English life was to be filled by drifting friends and bridge, which she played interminably, chain-smoking the while.

29. *Study of boats, South of France*, mid-1930s. Collection: The National Trust, Chartwell

30. *Swimming pool at Les Zoraïdes, Cap Martin,* c. 1935.
Collection: Mr and Mrs Russell S. Reynolds, Jnr. of Greenwich, Connecticut

But as the thirties opened, and in what was to be the last decade of her life, Maxine turned her back on Paris. Regaining much of her zest for life, she created a new house for herself at Golfe-Juan, near Cannes: Le Château de l'Horizon. The site was a veritable shelf of rock, which she had caused to be blasted out of the cliffside between the railway, the road and the sea. The white house was spacious and the acme of comfort; from the swimming pool was a water-chute down which bathers slid to the sea. Here, in her shining new domain, Maxine held court once more: the basic house party would be seven or eight, while other friends flocked to luncheon or dinner. The 'great days at Hartsbourne' found an echo here.

In 1933 Winston and Clementine visited Maxine for the first time in her new home. Between now and the outbreak of the Second World War, Winston was to come to the Château de l'Horizon another five times. He would usually be on his own, although Diana and Randolph accompanied him once; Clementine would only be with him on one further occasion. There were several reasons for her rather marked absenteeism. Apart from that first winter of 1922–3 at Cannes, which the family had so greatly enjoyed, and the visits she paid the Balsans at Lou Sueil, Clementine had come to dislike the Riviera. She used to say (rather perversely) that it was 'the climate', and that she never really 'felt well there'. Time did nothing to change her feelings about this popular sunlit playground. Nearly thirty years on, writing to Sarah from the Hôtel de Paris in Monte Carlo, where she and Winston were staying, she exclaimed: 'God – the Riviera is a ghastly place, I expect it's all right if you keep a flower shop or if you're a waiter!'[4]

Clementine liked going to Lou Sueil because she was fond of Jacques and Consuelo, and found the tenor of life and the company there most agreeable; but she did not like Maxine, whom she regarded as a snob and a vulgarian, and she abhorred the life of idleness, cards and gossip at the Château de l'Horizon, with people whom generally she thought boring and shallow. The same disadvantages (from her point of view) applied in varying degrees to Winston's other ports of call along the coast: to Les Zoraïdes at Cap Martin, for instance, where Winston liked staying with Daisy Fellowes.* Daisy was elegant, hard and predatory, and Clementine had long been wary of her.

Another hospitable house at Cap Martin was La Dragonnière, belonging to Lord Rothermere; he was a younger brother of Lord Northcliffe, who owned the *Daily Mail* and *Evening News*. Here Winston found most beautiful painting subjects in the olive groves and in the garden; but once again

---

* A daughter of the fourth Duc de Decazes. After the death of her first husband, Prince Jean de Broglie, she had married Reginald Fellowes, a kinsman of Winston's on the Spencer-Churchill side.

31. *On the Var, South of France,* c. 1935. Collection: The Hon. Julian Sandys

Clementine was not really in her milieu, and felt, reflecting upon life in the South of France in general, 'suffocated by luxury & ennui. . .'[5]

How was it therefore that Winston, with his keen mind and passion for political discussion, tolerated all this? For he did not suffer fools gladly, and was certainly not a socialite. The fact is that wherever he stayed he largely led his own life, and his indulgent (and indeed sensible) hosts excused him the normal duties of attendance and 'joining in' which are expected of most guests.

Maxine Elliott was known as an autocratic hostess, but Winston was free to lead the life he chose and to come and go as he pleased. 'She knew perfectly well', Diana Forbes-Robertson, Maxine's niece, was to write,

> that he, though out of office, towered above the familiars of the Château who came and went. He was the only person I saw permitted to be late for meals, and the only one who could leave the Château to paint at Saint Paul de Vence all day without being scolded as a 'gadabout'. Climbers who came to see the house were lazily tolerated by Maxine most of the time, but none were allowed to come and gawk at Churchill. He was a link with 'the great days at Hartsbourne', a reminder that she carried within her the knowledge of better times. There was no longer Curzon to raise his haughty head . . . There was no more Rosebery to yawn with boredom or flash with wit; no 'F.E.' to match against Winston; no Arthur Balfour with a languid leg draped over the chair arm, nor the old Prime Minister himself, Mr. Asquith ('Always looked like a high-class butler,' said Maxine). Winston and herself remembered days when many of the people who adorned her pool could not have entered any of the houses they knew in common. At the dinner party for the Windsors Winston remarked to Maxine in an undertone, 'What a lot of *ci-devants* we are here tonight,' and she smiled without rancour, proud to belong to a period that was past.[6]

Winston was welcome in her house (as in others) on his own terms: he would usually come accompanied by his valet and a secretary – for on holiday though he might have been, he was nearly always working steadily to meet some imminent deadline with his publishers. So part of the sunlit day would be spent, probably in bed in the morning, working at his proofs. After a swim there would be luncheon by the pool, then a painting expedition. Before dinner or afterwards, he would play mah-jong or bezique with his hostess; Winston greatly enjoyed these games as a small slice of the day. Then there was the lure of the Casino – another reason why Clementine dreaded this magic coast. Winston loved to gamble, and quite often lost more than he should.

As to personalities: Winston was easier-going than Clementine (who had a fierce Puritan streak in her) and he was very fond of Maxine; although by now she was very fat, and had snow-white hair, her head still had a commanding beauty and her eyes were large and expressive. Winston also admired her pluck, and the way she had made her way from insignificant beginnings to the top of the tree she had desired to climb. Half American himself, he instinctively liked her straightforwardness and found her congenial company. Perhaps beneath the layers of sophistication and elegant manners, learned rather than bred, there was a streak of that buccaneer spirit which he found so attractive.

We get glimpses of Château life in some of his letters to Clementine. In 1934 he and Randolph were staying with Maxine, who was evidently feeling the pinch:

> We brought good weather with us, & I am in my old room. . . I am afraid that Maxine is greatly impoverished by the American slump, & the $ exchange. She had $150,000 a year – she now has only $48,000. It is painful to her, after having worked so hard, & at last built herself exactly the home she wanted. Her theatre is shut up, & even so costs $22,000 a year in rates & taxes. So she is closing down this place in September & going to travel. . .[7]

Clementine, who was holidaying in Scotland, was only mildly sympathetic: 'Please give Maxine my love,' she wrote back. 'It is grievous after a life of hard work to lose two thirds of one's income. Still £10,000 a year is not too bad for a single woman!'[8]

Of his visit in the late summer of 1935 Winston wrote:

My darling,

   A variety of reasons induced me to stay here one more day. First: It gives me time to send you a letter as a herald! Second: I was rather successful last night at Baccarat: & Third: Finishing a beautiful picture: Fourth: the general optimism & contentment engendered by old Brandy after a luncheon here alone with Maxine in the conservatory instead of the concrete pool – of wh I am tired . . . so I exercised the privilege of changing my plans . . .

   I have now completed four pictures wh are I think superior in accomplishment to any I have done. Nich's [William Nicholson's] influence has been a great help. I thought perhaps you wd like to ask him for Sunday . . . here I have been so idle that I have done nothing but paint from morning to night. I have to stand up all the time, because of indigestion, so you can imagine how my legs ache . . . My darling, I trust that this letter will act as my ambassador & that I shall not be rebuked for not having written before. Really I have been utterly careless of the time: & have painted ferociously both out of doors & in my bedroom. Late for everything![9]

There was another observant and perceptive witness to life at the Château de l'Horizon in the person of James Vincent Sheean: in his mid-thirties, he was an American foreign correspondent who married Diana Forbes-Robertson in 1935. Soon after their marriage they arrived at the Château and found there, among the other guests, Winston Churchill. Over the next few years the visits of Sheean and his wife were again to coincide with Churchill's, and Sheean's book *Between the Thunder and the Sun*, which is a fascinating account of the European scene in the years of Hitler's rise to power, gives an account of life at Maxine's house and the varied company that was to be found there.

Sheean quickly spotted that Churchill was a strange figure among the polyglot, ramshackle collection of café–society figures who were his fellow guests:

> Winston in such a society was slightly out of place – more so even than Maxine – but he never noticed. He went to the South of France for a holiday and he proposed to take it as it happened, accepting whatever company there was, amiably bent upon making the best of everything. Nobody ever had such a lordly way of disregarding what seemed trivial or without significance. He could sit through a whole conversation on some subject that held no interest for him, and not a word of it would penetrate.[10]

During the summer of 1935 world events loomed large in Churchill's mind. Probably Vincent Sheean was one of the few present who listened to, or understood, his deep preoccupations:

> Mr. Churchill, in spite of the fact that he was on holiday, painting and taking the sun, could not keep his mind off these ominous foreshadows of the day of reckoning. He spoke constantly of the Ethiopian crisis, of the League, of Mussolini, of relations between England and Italy, of Italy's relations with Germany, and of German rearmament. . .[11]

Churchill assumed his hearers followed what he was saying, but a number of them probably found him a great bore. Sheean remarked that Winston could be surprisingly patient and tolerant:

> I well remember one day at lunch (a crowded lunch with thirty or forty people, on the terrace above the swimming-pool) when Mme. X,

scratching the inside of her shapely bare legs, inquired in a piercing nasal voice: 'Winston, why is it they always seem to go to *Geneva* for their meetings? Seems to me they could pick out a nicer place.'

Mr. Churchill paused in his mastication, looked at her benevolently from the shade of his big straw hat, and said, as to a child:

'Because, my dear, Geneva happens to be the seat of the League of Nations. You have heard of it, no doubt?'[12]

Sheean was interested in Churchill's attitude to his painting:

Mr. Churchill was painting a great deal that summer (1935) and used to spend every afternoon up in the hills, mainly at Saint-Pol. I always thought his painting showed a definite, although untaught and inexperienced, talent . . . True, the painting was interesting most of all because it had been done by him, but if it had been the work of a young man I believe it might have been said to show promise. He did it frankly as a hobby; he attached no importance at all to it, and laughed at anybody who pretended to take it seriously. But he did work at it and it gave him great pleasure. In this way it occupied a sort of intermediate place between writing – which he took very seriously, although it was not the prime business of his life – and bricklaying; it engaged his mind, perceptions and sense of form, although not his creative ambition, and had for him the advantages both of work (like writing) and of a simple pastime (like bricklaying).[13]

The year 1935 was the Silver Jubilee of King George V and Queen Mary; it also saw Stanley Baldwin succeed Ramsay MacDonald as Prime Minister (for the third time) in the National Government. There was now a possibility, although Churchill discounted it, that he might be offered a ministry: he was not. At the end of October Parliament was dissolved and there was a General Election, as a result of which the position of Baldwin and the Conservatives was greatly strengthened; speculation and rumours were rife in the home and foreign press and in political circles that now a place would certainly be found for Churchill. It was not. He did not delude himself as to his disappointment (which many people shared), and wrote some years later: 'This was to me a pang, and, in a way, an insult. There was much mockery in the Press. I do not pretend that, thirsting to get things on the move, I was not distressed. Lots of people have gone through this before, and will again.'[14]

Winston and Clementine already had a winter holiday planned, and now there was no need to curtail it. They left England on 10 December for Spain, visiting first Majorca and then Barcelona. Here their ways parted on about 20 December, for Clementine headed for home to spend Christmas and the rest of the school holidays with me (now thirteen), while Winston and 'the Prof' set out by boat for Tangier. Winston wanted to explore the painting possibilities in North Africa, which had been much recommended to him by various friends, several of whom, including Lord Rothermere, planned to be there at the same time. Tangier was emphatically not a success as it rained all the time, so Winston spent a rather miserable Christmas there thinking wistfully of Clementine and me, who were staying at Blenheim. He resolved to go to Marrakech in search of better weather; on the way there he wrote at length to Clementine from Rabat on 26 December, telling her he was working 'vy hard at Marlborough' and adding:

> I am longing to hear yr news from London & from Blenheim. I felt a little sad & lonely when I realised with a shock that it was Christmas Eve. I suppose you and Maria are now about to set off to Switzerland [actually Austria]. I do hope you will find it all you hope, & will not be too venturesome on the skis. . .

He ended this letter:

> My sweet darling I send you my fondest love and many many kisses from your wandering, sun-seeking, rather disconsolate W.[15]

Winston's spirits were soon cheered by the sunshine which greeted him in Marrakech. He stayed at the Mamounia Hotel, as he was to do so many times in future years, and wrote in enthusiastic terms about its comfortable rooms and excellent service and food.

His bedroom had a large balcony, and in a long letter to Clementine on 30 December he described the

> truly remarkable panorama over the tops of orange trees and olives, and the houses and ramparts of the native Marrakech, and like a great wall to the westward the snowclad range of the Atlas mountains – some of them are nearly fourteen thousand feet high. The light at dawn and sunset upon the snows, even at sixty miles distance, is as good as any snowscape I have ever seen.

He often painted views of the town from his balcony because, as he wrote to Clementine, 'although the native city is full of attractive spots, the crowds, the smells and the general discomfort for painting have repelled me'.[16] But, as we know from many of his canvases, he did also paint in and around the town itself.

Winston did not want for lively and agreeable company: Randolph had

32. *Marrakech, December 1935–January 1936.* Collection: The National Trust, Chartwell

joined his father and 'the Prof'; Lord Rothermere and his party were there; and so was Lloyd George, who was busy writing a book. Political preoccupations were grave, and conversation and letters were full of the consequences of the infamous Hoare–Laval Pact, by which the Foreign Ministers of Britain and France had met secretly in Paris in early December and agreed a compromise solution to the Abyssinian war. The agreement had leaked and caused an uproar, as it undermined Britain's policy of support for the League of Nations, and was to the disadvantage of Abyssinia.

On a family note, Winston was concerned by Randolph's intention to accept the invitation of the Unionist Association of the Ross and Cromarty

33. *Marrakech, December 1935–January 1936.* Collection: The Lady Soames, DBE

constituency to stand in a by-election pending there. He was to be their candidate against Malcolm MacDonald (Ramsay's son), who was a Cabinet Minister in the National Government. Winston felt that this would be regarded as a form of continuing hostility, inspired by himself, against the Baldwin government; it came, moreover, at a time when he still thought he might be offered a place. His letters to Clementine were full of these matters, as well as of accounts of his painting and reports of progress on the third volume of *Marlborough*. Indeed he was very productive during these holiday weeks. When 'the Prof' returned home to England during the first week in January, he bore with him three draft chapters; Winston had also written some newspaper articles and completed seven pictures.

Randolph returned home too, to present himself for the fight in Ross and Cromarty despite parental qualms. But Winston was not left alone. Diana and her husband Duncan Sandys, whom she had married the previous autumn, arrived to keep him company. Winston reported to Clementine that he was very happy in his new haven, and had no definite plans to return home for a while. He depicted a charming scene of family contentment when he wrote to her on 8 January 1936:

> It is vy nice having Diana & Duncan here. They are so happy. They say it is a second honeymoon . . . The more I see of him, the better I like him. They read political books to each other under the palm trees while I paint.[17]

In the middle of January Winston and his party left Marrakech to reconnoitre Meknes and Fez, which lie about 250 miles to the north. They had heard a good deal about the beauty and interest of these places. But they returned a few days later, for although Winston thought Meknes and its environs pleasant and very healthy, he deemed them 'far less paintable and romantic',[18] and far less warm, than Marrakech, to which he returned with pleasure. He expected to spend a little more time there, but on 20 January King George V died; Churchill therefore ended his holiday and set out for home, where he was invited to present the Address of the House to King Edward VIII upon his accession.

This long winter holiday in the sunshine had been a great success, and was marked chiefly by Winston's discovery of Marrakech; it had delighted him in every way, and he had told Clementine how much he wished she could have been there with him: 'I must say I should like to take you there some day. . .'[19] That day would come, for in later years Marrakech remained a favourite place for him, and offered an ample supply of scenes for his brush.

CHAPTER SEVEN

Although Winston's principal genre was landscapes, he also painted a considerable number of still lifes, flower paintings and interiors, as well as portraits. Forced indoors by the weather, he would look around him for subjects. Members of his family or friends would advise, or hurry to help him compose a 'paintatious' group. It might be a 'bottlescape' like the one that hangs in the dining room at Chartwell today – an array of assorted bottles, from a gargantuan bottle of brandy to an imperial pint of champagne flanked with cigar boxes, lit by a lamp; or a study in silver and white and cream, composed from silver sugar urns, a salver and a tooth-pick box (p. 107); or a classic study group of a loaf of bread, fruit and a half-empty glass on a white tablecloth (p. 108). He had taken his first lesson in still-life painting when he had copied the Sargent in Philip Sassoon's collection, way back in the twenties.

In summertime it pleased Winston to paint flowers, and he so successfully captured the 'personalities' of some of his flower subjects that it makes one wish he had painted them more often. He was able to convey the silky texture of mallows, or the thick, creamy lusciousness of the flowers of the lemon-scented magnolia, contrasted with the polished boldness of its big leaves (pp. 106 and 109). These he loved to pick from the exceptionally tall specimen of *Magnolia grandiflora* Clementine had planted at the foot of the wall beneath his bedroom window.

While staying away with friends – with Philip Sassoon, for instance, at Port Lympne or Trent Park – he would often paint interior scenes. His *Blue Room at Trent*, painted in 1934, is a most striking picture of what must have been a luxuriously lovely room. While staying at Knebworth House with Lord and Lady Lytton (born Pamela Plowden, she was Winston's first great love from the far-off days in India, and they had always remained devoted friends), he painted the Great Hall, and this is where the picture hangs today.

Blenheim provided an infinity of subjects. He seems to have liked best of

34. *Mallows in a vase, Chartwell,* 1930s. Collection: The Countess Peel

35. *Still life: silver at Chartwell,* 1930s. Collection: The Countess of Avon

36. *A loaf of bread*, 1930s. Collection: Winston S. Churchill, MP

37. *Magnolia grandiflora, Chartwell*, 1930s. The Charles II silver-gilt vase
was one of a pair bequeathed to CSC by the Edwardian financier Sir Ernest Cassel in 1921.
Collection: The Lady Soames, DBE

38. *Tapestries at Blenheim Palace*, mid to late 1930s. Collection: The Lady Soames, DBE

all to paint inside the great house rather than out of doors, taking advantage of the unique and glorious subject matter there: the Long Library, the Great Hall; and, best of all, the tapestries depicting the campaigns of the Great Duke. His sumptuous painting *Tapestries at Blenheim Palace* (p. 110) was judged by Professor Thomas Bodkin, an art critic and writer of international repute, to be possibly Churchill's best interior.[1]

Winston always said he hated snow, but he painted it most successfully – though nearly always, it must be said, from the inside looking out, safely and warmly ensconced behind a window. When she was fifty Clementine, with much courage and dash, took up ski-ing – something she and I could do together in the Christmas holidays. Several times she tried to lure Winston to the snowy mountains, and in 1937 he almost succumbed. Winston was at Chartwell at the end of January when Clementine wrote from the Palace Hotel in St Moritz (I by then had been despatched back to school):

> My darling,
>
> I was overjoyed when I read your telegram saying that perhaps on your way to the Riviera you might join me here for a few days. Oh please do – I should love it so much & really I believe you would like this place. The air is like champagne & you could sit in the sun & paint without a great coat. You could paint the most fairy like pale dazzling pictures – The fir trees weighted down with sparkling snow are too beautiful – The snow itself is mauve pink & every shade of warm white . . .
>
> Then this hotel is extremely comfortable & cosmopolitan – The food is hot & good . . .[2]

On the eve of his departure with Randolph for the South of France, where they were going to stay at La Dragonnière with Lord Rothermere, Winston seemed all set to join Clementine at St Moritz: 'I am much looking forward to painting your lovely coloured snows on which Lavery, years ago, dilated and enthused me . . .'[3] But in the end the balmy sunshine of the Riviera won the day – much to Clementine's disappointment, but perhaps not totally to her surprise.

As the thirties rolled on, the march of events quickened: in early 1936 Hitler's forces occupied the demilitarized zone of the Rhineland; in early May the defeat and annexation by Italy of Abyssinia was completed; and in mid-July the Spanish Civil War broke out. In 1937, after the Coronation in May of King George VI and Queen Elizabeth, Stanley Baldwin retired. He was succeeded by Neville Chamberlain, and from now on appeasement would increasingly characterize the foreign policy of Britain's government.

In the last week of August 1936 Winston started his summer holiday

39. *Snow under the arch*, c. 1935. The subject of this picture is a mystery, and its date
is uncertain. It was probably painted from a photograph. CSC loved it, and
called it *The Messenger*. Collection: The Lady Soames, DBE

40. *Chartwell in winter*, late 1930s. This view from the house looks over Orchard
Cottage (right) and the Studio (left), and away over the Weald of Kent.
Collection: The Lady Soames, DBE

41. *Olive grove at La Dragonnière, Cap Martin*, 1937. Collection: The Lady Soames, DBE

abroad at St Georges-Motel, staying with the Balsans; he moved on from there to Maxine Elliott's Château de l'Horizon, where he enjoyed an agreeable and fruitful visit. He wrote to Clementine from here on 5 September:

> My darling,
>   I have been painting all day & every day. I have found a beautiful clear river – the Loup – & a quiet wild spot, & I study the clear water. I have done two variants which I hope you will admire as much as I do! Wow![4]

He was evidently in splendid spirits. Lord Lloyd, a parliamentary colleague who was visiting mutual friends, wrote to his son:

> 6th September 1936
>   Yesterday we went to lunch with Muriel Wilson at the villa near by. Winston had come over from Maxine Elliott's at the Château de l'Horizon at Cannes . . . to meet us at lunch. He arrived in an enormous Texan hat, the car full of easels & painting appliances plus the faithful Inches [his valet] and was in very good form. . .[5]

His holiday over, Winston attended to political affairs before returning home. He briefly visited a former French Prime Minister, and more recently Minister for Foreign Affairs, Pierre-Etienne Flandin at Domecy-sur-Cure, Yonne. From here he wrote to Clementine:

> The eleven days I passed with Maxine were pleasant – The weather beautiful, every comfort, & I have painted six beautiful pictures, besides the three at Dreux. I am sending them home tomorrow or next day by Mrs P.* but do not unpack them till I come: for I want to do the honours with them for yr benefit myself. . .[6]

That last sentence conjures up memories of many homecomings. On his return from holidays, my father would line up all the canvases he had painted around the room, usually standing on the floor and leaning against the furniture. Then he would make my mother sit next to him and show them to her, explaining where each picture had been painted and any problems he had had with it; other members of the family, and guests, would also be welcome at this 'exhibition' of his works. Naturally he hoped for praise and encouragement, which were generally forthcoming. Although my father was genuinely unconceited about his efforts as a painter (as many people have noticed) and although he sincerely asked for, and accepted, criticism and advice from professional artists, yet he did love to be praised

---

* Mrs Pearman, his secretary.

42. *The Loup River, Alpes Maritimes, 1936.*
Collection: The Tate Gallery; at present on loan to 10 Downing Street

43. *Scene on the River Loup, 1936.* Collection: The Hon. Mrs Celia Perkins

and 'petted' by his home audience. The writer Peter Quennell was most perceptive about this almost childlike wish for appreciation. When Quennell visited La Capponcina (Lord Beaverbrook's house at Cap d'Ail, where Winston often stayed after the war) in 1952, Churchill was there too:

A view of Mr Churchill's latest canvases closed this memorable afternoon. Asked his opinion of Mao Tse-Tung's poems. Arthur Waley observed that, in terms of aesthetic achievement, they were not quite so good as Churchill's pictures; and the series of landscapes I had seen around Randolph's London dining-room I had never much admired. Thanks to the expert tuition of William Nicholson and Paul Maze, he had lost his Sunday-painter's innocence; and the works he showed us at Cap Martin, with their bold brush-strokes and heavy splashes of colour, were more ambitious than appealing. While he displayed them, however, I beheld the heroic veteran from an unfamiliar point of view. Like all artists, good or bad, I suspected, he was sometimes plagued by doubts, and felt the sad discrepancy between what he had envisaged and the results he had produced. So splendidly confident in everything else he did, here he needed our support and hovered about us almost anxiously, showing picture after picture, while he awaited the words of appreciation that were often difficult to find.[7]

Clementine was Winston's best critic – although he was not always pleased with her judgements. She was really quite brave; I have seen her stand watching my father painting, and then suddenly quite calmly remove his canvas from the easel and walk off with it! One of her more frequent criticisms was that Winston was prone to 'overwork' a picture, and she would try to remove it at what she judged to be the moment when the best result had been achieved. No one else would have dreamed of taking such a liberty, and needless to say my father used sometimes to be very angry when she 'swooped' away his masterpiece. My mother also encouraged Winston to keep his palette 'cool' and 'à la Nicholson'. Although he sometimes grumbled, Winston always wanted to know what she thought, and paid considerable attention to her criticisms.

 The impressive tally of pictures to which Winston referred in his letter – all painted over a period of three weeks – was not achieved without a measure of stoicism and determination on his part. He had for some time been suffering from severe bouts of indigestion and had tried various remedies (including deep-breathing exercises). During this holiday he had written to Dr Thomas Hunt from St Georges-Motel, to say that

> I have had a good deal of indigestion since arriving here. Of course painting always tries me highly, but I cannot give it up on my holidays. It is the mental concentration which seems to affect the stomach. I always paint standing up, as otherwise the indigestion would be very severe. . .[8]

This tiresome ailment was prone to recur from time to time, and was perhaps symptomatic of stress or fatigue.

During these weeks, too, Churchill had witnessed the French army on manoeuvres, and before returning home he had visited the Maginot Line – France's much vaunted, and supposedly impassable, barrier against an invading army. Time and again one notices that Winston's holidays were rarely removed from the stern realities of the political scene, and the number of letters addressed to colleagues and others bear witness to the fact that for him 'out of sight' was most certainly not 'out of mind'.

During the later years of this decade Churchill endured a deep sense of frustration at not being allowed to play a role in the government of his country, for which he had no doubt he was well fitted. As for his writings, he was driven by both the feeling that time for such things was running out and the very real need to earn large sums of money, to support his lavish mode of living and sustain his family. All these factors may well have contributed to periods of gloom and depression. Around this time, Winston seriously contemplated selling his much loved home Chartwell; he discussed this unwelcome prospect in a letter to Clementine in February 1937, writing that although they could carry on for a year or two, 'no good offer should be refused, having regard to the fact that our children are almost all flown, and my life is probably in its closing decade'.[9] These last words have a strange ring for those who know the still long and splendid tale that had yet to unfold.

Such were the pressures of 1937 that, apart from ten days at La Dragonnière in February, Winston stayed mainly at Chartwell. He did have plans for his usual late-summer visit to Maxine Elliott, but regretfully had to telegraph her on 4 September: 'Thinking much of you all and the pool. Alas am tied here by work on Marlborough. If a chance comes later, will propose myself. Love, Winston.'[10] That year, no further chance did present itself. But although he was disappointed to miss his spell of Riviera sunshine he was always happy at home: it was lucky indeed that an offer for Chartwell never did materialize. When his old friend Bendor Westminster made contact with him later in September, Winston telegraphed him: 'So glad hear from you again. Am dwelling here in peace and health writing books and painting.'[11] The message seems to breathe contentment and tranquillity.

44. *The goldfish pool at Chartwell*, 1930s. Collection: The Lady Soames, DBE

But time was running out. As 1938 opened, eighteen more months remained of an uneasy peace. There would be time for just two more visits to the Château de l'Horizon, and one more to St Georges-Motel. Winston's visit to Maxine Elliott that January was as pleasant as ever. He divided his time abroad in two, leaving the Château for a short interlude at Les Zoraïdes. During his first lap at the Château, he wrote to Clementine on 10 January:

> I have been here nearly a week practically without quitting the house. I do not get up till luncheon time, but work in bed and have a masseur. After lunch we play Mah Jong till 5 o'clock, when I again retire to rest and work. I have not played bezique nor have I been to the Rooms. MJ has been amusing and very inexpensive. I have lost about £2 after all these hours of harmless amusement. I have not unpacked my painting things, nor indeed done anything of any sort or kind, except to dine once at the Windsors and once with Flandin.[12]

The dinners for the Windsors and others were, it appears, a great success; Maxine, Winston recounted,

> declared that she had not had such pleasant dinners since her great days at Hartsbourne, when she gathered political stars into her orbit. The Windsor-LG [Lloyd George] dinner was a great success, and the poor duke gay and charming although he had to fight for his place in the conversation like other people. . .[13]

Maxine Elliott's thoughts were of a glittering past which Winston too could well remember – but his preoccupations were with the present, and the grim future.

Later, most unusually, Clementine joined Winston at the Château de l'Horizon, after her now habitual ski-ing holiday with me. Winston, it seems, had persuaded her to make this graceful *acte de présence* – which would have greatly delighted him, for he always regretted that she would not come to these places which he enjoyed so much.

In March 1938 the *Anschluss* took place: German troops entered Vienna, and Austria was incorporated into the Reich. Czechoslovakia was next on the list. The traumas of the Munich crisis in September banished all holiday thoughts. As winter closed in Winston was working hard at his books and politics. Clementine had had rather a bad year health-wise, and went off in November for a sea voyage to the West Indies in Lord Moyne's boat, the *Rosaura*. Four years earlier, in the autumn of 1934, she and Winston had sailed with Lord Moyne through the Eastern Mediterranean; some lovely canvases of Greek temples and a sunlit prospect of the battlements at

45. *Ruined Greek temple, 1934.* Collection: The Lady Soames, DBE

46. *The ramparts at Rhodes, 1934*. Collection: Winston S. Churchill, MP

Rhodes survive from this trip. But Winston no longer felt able to go on cruises of this kind – they took him too far away, and too far out of touch.

In January 1939 Winston went to stay at the Château de l'Horizon for the last time; for this was to prove the last year of Maxine's life. As usual he wrote often to Clementine. He reported that although the sunshine was radiant, there was a nip in the air; he would stay two weeks at the Château, and work hard at his book. As the weather deteriorated it was not propitious for painting, but this visit was particularly good for writing: 'I have stayed in bed every morning and made great progress with the book. We [he and his secretary] have averaged fifteen hundred words a day, although

123

nominally on holiday . . .'[14] Social life was highlighted by the Windsors' dining 'here and we dine back with them . . .'

Vincent and Diana Sheean were also staying with Maxine. Sheean, radical in his views, strongly supported the Spanish Republicans, who were being savagely defeated by Franco's forces. Nevertheless, in the politically reactionary society of the Riviera, Churchill and the Sheeans found themselves in sympathy in realizing the deadly danger the dictators represented. On his arrival Winston had said to Diana: 'We're all together now.'[15]

The euphoria of the thousands throughout the country who had cheered the Munich Agreement was followed by the growing realization that it had only bought us time to try and catch up on the wasted years in building Britain's defences. Many people listened to Churchill and his supporters now, and began to accept the truth of what they had been saying about the deadly dangers which confronted Britain and France. As for those who still believed in the fragile peace which had been bought at such a high price, their confidence was rudely shattered when in March 1939 Germany annexed what remained of independent Czechoslovakia. Less than a month later, on Good Friday, Italy marched into Albania.

From April onwards, calls for Churchill to be included in the Government came from all sides, and were featured almost daily in the press; but they fell on obstinately deaf ears. Winston himself stepped up the pace of his work on the *English-Speaking Peoples*, in his determination to meet his agreed delivery date. At the same time he did not relax in his campaign, waged in the press and in Parliament, to pressurize the Government into taking all measures necessary and possible for national security. In a telling phrase in May he warned that 'the glare of Nazi Germany is to be turned on Poland'.[16] People were beginning now – at this late hour – to listen to his prophecies.

In August visitors to Chartwell found Winston toiling at the last stages of his book, grimly convinced that war was now imminent. On 14 August he flew to France once more, to visit the Rhine section of the Maginot Line; then he joined up with Clementine and myself (now nearly seventeen, and having just left school for good) for a visit to Jacques and Consuelo Balsan at St Georges-Motel: it was to be a brief enough interlude.

In his war memoirs, Winston was to recall that last holiday of peacetime.

On my return from the Rhine front I passed some sunshine days at Madame Balsan's place, with a pleasant but deeply anxious company, in the old Château, where King Henry of Navarre had slept the night

47. *The Thames at Taplow*, late 1930s. Taplow Court, Buckinghamshire, was the home of Lord and Lady Desborough. Collection: The National Trust, Chartwell

before the battle of Ivry. Mrs Euan Wallace and her sons* were with us. Her husband was a Cabinet Minister. She was expecting him to join her. Presently he telegraphed he could not come, and would explain later why. Other signs of danger drifted in upon us. One could feel the deep apprehension brooding over all, and even the light of this lovely valley at the confluence of the Eure and the Vesgre seemed robbed of its genial ray. I found painting hard work in this uncertainty.[17]

Paul Maze and his family were there, living in the Moulin de Montreuil; he and Winston painted the same agreeable scene of the old mill house with the millstream swirling past. In his diary for 20 August, Maze wrote:

> Winston came to paint the Moulin. I worked alongside him. He suddenly turned to me and said: 'This is the last picture we shall paint in peace for a very long time.' What amazed me was his concentration over his painting. No one but he could have understood more what the possibility of war meant, and how ill prepared we were. As he worked, he would now and then make statements as to the relative strengths of the German Army or the French Army. 'They are strong, I tell you, they are strong,' he would say. Then his jaw would clench his large cigar, and I felt the determination of his will. 'Ah' he would say, 'with it all, we shall have him.'[18]

During the thirties, Winston and Clementine had often stayed with the Balsans, in this beautiful rose-brick, slate-roofed, sixteenth-century house surrounded by its deep, wide moat; they always found the company congenial, and Winston never lacked for subjects to paint in the park and garden. On one occasion he was absorbed in painting a view of the long canal, overshadowed by trees, from the lawn in front of the house. Consuelo had that day invited Paul Maze and three other artists to luncheon; observing the amateur at work, they crowded round him to inspect his picture. In her memoirs, Mme Balsan described how, undaunted by the presence of experts, Winston

> drew four brushes from his stock and handing them round said, 'You, Paul, shall paint the trees – you, Segonzac,† the sky – you, Simon Lévy,‡ the water and you, Marchand,§ the foreground, and I shall supervise.' Thus I later found them busily engaged. Winston, smoking

---

* Of her five sons and stepsons, three would be killed on active service.

† A. Dunoyer de Segonzac (1884–1974), French painter and engraver.

‡ Simon Lévy, or Simon-Lévy (b.1886), French portrait- and landscape-painter.

§ Probably Jean Marchand (1883–1940), French painter and engraver.

48. *The château at St Georges-Motel*, mid to late 1930s. Collection: The Hon. Mrs Celia Perkins

49. *In the park of the château at St Georges-Motel*, mid-1930s. The painting is signed
by Paul Maze, A.D. de Segonzac, WSC, Simon Lévy, Ivor Spencer-Churchill and Jacques Balsan,
all of whom contributed to it. This is a real curiosity! Private Collection

a big cigar, a critical eye on the progress of his picture, now and then intervened – 'a little more blue here in your sky, Segonzac – your water more shadowed, Lévy – and, Paul, your foliage a deeper green just there.' It was all I could do to drag them away to luncheon.[19]

The final version of the picture – which, one has to admit, bears out the truth of the saying 'Too many cooks spoil the broth' – was signed not only by the artists already mentioned and Winston, but also by Jacques Balsan and Ivor Spencer-Churchill, who were not able to resist the temptation to have a hand in so remarkable a composition.

An example of the lengths to which Winston would go for the sake of his painting also belongs to St Georges-Motel. On one of his visits there he decided he wanted to paint the moat with ripples on the water, and since there was no obliging breeze two gardeners were asked to row a boat to the appropriate place and create ripples with the oars. A photographer had also been sent for from Dreux, to record the scene for the artist's future reference. Mme Balsan wrote:

I can still see the scene with Winston personally directing the manoeuvre – the photographer running around to do snapshots – the gardeners clumsily belabouring the water. With characteristic thoroughness Winston persisted until all possibilities had been exhausted and the photographer, hot and worried, could be heard muttering, '*Mais ces Anglais sont donc tous maniac.*'[20]

Those were happy, carefree memories; but I remember so well that visit in August 1939. The weather was glorious, and the scene surrounding us pleasant and peaceful; life at the Château represented the peak of elegance and civilization; but we all felt threatened. I recall too that not all was harmony among the company, one or two of whom were hostile to my father's political views and to Britain. Paul Maze has described how, while he was talking to my father, one of the other English guests shouted down from the stairs, 'Don't listen to him. He is a warmonger.'[21]

The news was becoming increasingly grave and Winston felt he must return home, so he took his leave on 23 August, less than a week after his arrival; my mother and I were to follow him shortly after. His private secretary, Mary Shearburn, travelled back with him to England, and took his dictation in the car between Dreux and Paris. When he had finished

he lapsed into silence, and she sat looking out of the window at the beautiful and peaceful country through which they were passing. The corn was ripe and, in its heaviness, it looked like the golden waves of a gently undulating sea.

50. *Unfinished study of the goldfish pool at Chartwell*, mid to late 1930s.
Collection: The National Trust, Chartwell

Mr Churchill grew graver and graver as he sat wrapped in thought, and then said slowly and sorrowfully:

'Before the harvest is gathered in – we shall be at war.'[22]

130

CHAPTER EIGHT

On 1 September 1939 the Germans invaded Poland; two days later Great Britain and France declared war on Germany. On that same day Neville Chamberlain invited Winston Churchill to join his Government, and to be First Lord of the Admiralty. The Board of Admiralty signalled the Fleet: 'Winston is back!'

He received many letters rejoicing at his appointment, among them one from Paul Maze, who wrote from the Moulin de Montreuil on 3 September:

> I feel happy to know that the responsibility of the Navy is in your hands at this juncture.
>
> I am writing this only a few yards from the spot where your easel stood ten days ago . . .[1]

There was no more time or thought for painting now. Chartwell would soon be shut up, although for a time Winston and Clementine would use Orchard House, the small house next door to the Studio at the bottom of the orchard: Winston himself had built much of it during the last months of peace.

In the spring of 1940 came personal news that saddened Winston: Maxine Elliott had died on 5 March, aged seventy-three. Winston arranged for George Keppel (another figure from that glossy Edwardian age which seemed even more remote now), who was still living on the Riviera, to represent him at Maxine's funeral; she was buried in the Protestant Cemetery at Cannes. Docteur Brés, her devoted friend and doctor, wrote to Winston and said that on the morning of her death she had spoken of him: 'Winston knows how to take his responsibilities,' she had said. 'Nothing can frighten him – he should be Prime Minister.'[2]

At dawn on 10 May 1940 the German hordes assaulted Holland, Belgium and Luxembourg. That evening Winston Churchill received the King's commission to form a National Government.

Winston was to paint just one picture during the nearly five-year period of the war in Europe; that was in January 1943, after the Conference of the 'Big Two' – Roosevelt and Churchill – and their closest military and political advisers at Casablanca in Morocco. The Conference lasted some ten days, and, as the American President prepared to depart, Winston said to him:

> You cannot go all this way to North Africa without seeing Marrakech. Let us spend two days there. I must be with you when you see the sunset on the snows of the Atlas Mountains.[3]

Winston had not forgotten the beauties of the place which had so captivated him in the winter of 1935–6, and he beguiled the President with a vivid description of Marrakech:

> 'the Paris of the Sahara' where all the caravans had come from Central Africa for centuries to be heavily taxed *en route* by the tribes in the mountains and afterwards swindled in the Marrakesh markets, receiving the return, which they greatly valued, of the gay life of the city, including fortune-tellers, snake-charmers, masses of food and drink, and on the whole the largest and most elaborately organised brothels in the African continent.[4]

The President allowed himself to be persuaded by Winston's colourful enthusiasm, and so on 24 January they drove in convoy with their respective personal entourages the hundred and fifty miles to Marrakech, a journey which took four hours. On the way they paused for a picnic luncheon in the wild and open desert. The party consisted of nearly thirty people, and while they ate, armoured cars patrolled around them, secret servicemen kept close guard with loaded Tommy guns, and vigilant aircraft circled overhead. This must surely rank as one of the more bizarre picnics ever to be recorded.[5]

When they arrived at their destination, Roosevelt and Churchill stayed with the American Vice-Consul, whose residence was a most delightful house lent by a rich American, Mrs Moses Taylor. The house had been designed on indigenous lines, with a central courtyard with orange trees and fountains. From its Berber tower there was a beautiful view over the town of Marrakech, away to the Atlas Mountains. At the magic hour the President was carried up the winding stairs of the tower by two of his servants (who made a chair with their arms), and the two friends sat and watched the sun set in all its glory behind the distant snowy peaks.

The President left for the United States early the next morning; Winston, who wished to bid him farewell, was late in getting out of bed, so he came down in his brilliant dressing-gown – red with gold dragons. On an impulse he got into the President's car in this unconventional attire and drove with him to the airfield.

51. *A view of Marrakech, with the tower of the Katoubia mosque, January 1943.*
This was the only picture WSC painted during the war.
Collection: The late Norman G. Hickman, DSC, of New York City

133

After the President's departure, Winston returned to the Villa Taylor and got out his paints: he must have hoped even before leaving England that this dream might come true. Lord Moran, his doctor, who always accompanied him abroad, described how he climbed up the tower again and spent a long time gazing in silence at the view. 'He seemed reluctant to break the illusion of a holiday,'[6] wrote Lord Moran in his diary, 'which for a few hours has given him a chance to get his breath.' Then he set to work to paint. He later gave the finished picture to President Roosevelt, as a memento of this short interlude in the crash of war (p. 133).

It was not long before Churchill was in Marrakech again, but the circumstances were very different, and this time there was to be no painting. After the Tehran Conference in late November 1943, when the 'Big Three' met for the first time (and when he celebrated his sixty-ninth birthday), Churchill left to return to England by way of Cairo and Tunis. He had not been well since he left home, but by the time he arrived in Carthage he found he could go no further: he had pneumonia. General Eisenhower hospitably made his nearby villa, The White House, available to him. Sarah was already with Winston, having accompanied him on the journey as his ADC, and Clementine now flew out too. They all spent that Christmas at Carthage. Although from the moment he possibly could, Winston had resumed working – much to the disapproval of his doctors – they and Clementine insisted that he must have a proper period of convalescence before returning to England. Once more Marrakech cast its benign and magic spell; the Villa Taylor was again made available, and Winston, Clementine and Sarah lived there for some three weeks. He made a steady recovery, and insisted upon quickly resuming his conduct of the war and receiving politicians and service commanders. He was able to go for picnics (in more congenial sites than he and the President had found on their way from Casablanca), but to his disappointment he did not find the strength to paint.

In the late spring and early summer of 1945 the mounting tidal wave of Allied victory surged across Europe – east to west: west to east – at once liberating and destructive. It heaped up flotsam and jetsam which years of hindsight and bitter enquiry would fail to disentangle.

At home the party-political truce strained at its bonds, and although the war in the Far East still raged, the Labour and Liberal parties withdrew from the wartime coalition. Churchill formed a Caretaker Conservative Government to tide over the interval which must elapse before a General Election could be held.

Probably for the first time in his life, he was not entirely in his element at the hustings. Nearly five years of all-party collaboration, and a patriotic unity of purpose in the nation, made it hard for him at first to attune once more to the acerbities of party politics, and his own 'feel' for the fisticuffs of electioneering seemed at first to have deserted him. The great tours he made throughout the length and breadth of the country saw vast crowds who cheered him to the echo; very few, either in his own circle or in the press, foresaw the political debacle which lay around the corner.

A unique feature characterized this Election: in order to allow the Service votes from the most remote parts of the globe to be flown back to Britain and counted, there was a delay of three weeks between Polling Day on 5 July and the count and declaration of the poll. During this interval a meeting of the Big Three at Potsdam was planned to start – a meeting which would overlap with the results of the British General Election. President Roosevelt had died suddenly on 12 April, less than a month before victory in Europe, and his successor, President Truman, was anxious to meet Stalin and Churchill. Urgent decisions were needed, moreover, concerning the problems and perils victory brought in her train. To while away the short interval between Polling Day and the beginning of the Conference, it was planned that Winston and Clementine should have a holiday – their first since the outbreak of war. The arrangements had to be quick and simple, and the place could not be too far-flung, or recently ravaged by the war. They chose the area in France south of Bordeaux, and a Canadian, Brigadier-General Brutinel, invited Winston and his party to stay at his house, the Château de Bordaberry near St Jean-de-Luz. Mr Bryce Nairn, the British Consul at Bordeaux, helped a great deal with the arrangements; he and his delightful wife Margaret (who had been a professional painter before her marriage) had already met Winston and Clementine, for in the winter of 1943–4 when Winston was recovering from his illness at Marrakech, Bryce Nairn was Consul there. Both Winston and Clementine had liked the Nairns very much, and their presence nearby for this holiday was an added pleasure and advantage.

The party consisted of Winston and Clementine, myself (on special leave from the ATS), Lord Moran, Jock Colville (Private Secretary on duty and an admirable companion), two secretaries, a detective, and Winston's valet Sawyers. We all left London on 7 July. Bordaberry is a comfortable, plain white 'manor' house, looking over the Bay of Biscay where a tongue of land at the mouth of the Bidassoa separates Spain from France. Our host was a most interesting man; of French-Canadian descent, and formerly a high-ranking officer in the Canadian army, he was a naturalized Frenchman and the owner of Château Margaux vineyard. Remaining in France throughout the war, he had taken a leading part in helping Allied airmen and prisoners-of-war to escape across the Pyrenees into Spain. General Brutinel and Winston were soon on the best of terms, and their budding friendship was greatly fostered by the fact that they had both, during the First World War at 'Plugstreet', heard a character known as 'Foghorn MacDonald' swear – apparently a never-to-be-forgotten experience.

At first Winston was tired, crotchety and restless, and could not get started on painting. The unusual circumstance of being suddenly 'at leisure', and the weird feeling which was common to us all – that we were in suspended animation while the ballot boxes held their secret – combined to make it hard for him to settle down. On our second afternoon, however, when we went to visit the Nairns at St Jean-de-Luz, things looked up, for once we had been guided by Margaret Nairn to a good 'paintatious' spot the Muse took charge, and Winston began to paint. 'He has laid his first picture,' I reported in my diary, 'and we are all delighted.' Now that my father was happily ensconced and occupied, my mother and I spent the afternoon 'being rolled and tossed by the breakers at St. Jean de Luz – while halfway up the hill, Papa in sombrero and beneath a mushroom umbrella, puffed and painted . . . '[7]

From then on the holiday flowed in an agreeable sequence of painting sorties, although the painting at St Jean-de-Luz was interrupted by a violent thunderstorm on its second day. Another time we all made an expedition up the river Nivelle, from the bank of which Winston painted a house and surrounding scenery on the opposite side. On one occasion he sat so long – four hours or so – at his easel that it brought on an attack of troublesome indigestion.

Margaret Nairn would pitch her own easel not far from Winston and was available for advice and encouragement. When they painted the same view, Winston would contemplate the two versions intently; he liked Mrs Nairn very much, admired her painting and enjoyed discussing artistic problems with her. While these sessions were in progress the rest of the party passed the time in pleasant and peaceful occupations: we too were savouring the first days of peace.

Bathing on the vast expanse of the beach at Hendaye was quite a carefully stage-managed performance, which I described in my diary on 12 July:

Papa came down and bathed for the first time. We had a tent pitched à la Sultan, half way down the beach – from which Papa emerged in shapeless drawers – smoking and with his ten gallon hat on – Sawyers un-crowned and un-cigared him as he took to the waves. I was so happy to see Papa – floating peacefully like a charming porpoise, washed by translucent waves . . .

The previous November Winston Churchill and General de Gaulle had walked together down the Champs-Elysées from the Arc de Triomphe, and all Paris had gone mad with joy and exultation; wherever Churchill had been received in the city during the two days of his official visit he had received a tumultuous welcome. Now on this quiet and unofficial holiday visit to a provincial region of France, nothing was too much trouble for anyone if it 'would please *le grand* Churchill'. The mayors and local Resistance leaders and other dignitaries combined to present a programme of Basque dancing and *pelota Basque* at the Château de Bordaberry; it must be confessed that the programme was rather long, and Winston was secretly longing to paint, but the warmth of their intention was greatly appreciated. On another evening our whole party attended a fireworks display (including a *toro fuego*) at Hendaye, where Winston was received with rapturous applause. But most touching of all were the little groups of people, including children, who would appear it seemed from nowhere whenever the now well-known, and unmistakable, form of their hero was descried – to greet him with cheers and waves and clapping, or to stand quite quietly, at a discreet distance, watching him paint.

This agreeable and truly well-earned holiday lasted a little more than a week, during which Winston seemed most of the time quite unusually content to be far removed from the scene of action. Of course if it was necessary he could be swiftly in touch with Number 10, and had with him a member of his Private Office (Jock Colville) and a secretary. During that holiday, however, he sent only one telegram and one minute, and showed little desire to be closely *au courant* with events. One message of prime importance was conveyed to him during these days, and Jock Colville described how

> Before we left for France Churchill asked President Truman to telegraph the result of the test of the first atomic bomb shortly due to take place in the Nevada desert. 'Let me know,' he had signalled, 'whether it is a flop or a plop.' When we were about to leave Bordaberry a telegram came from the President to the Prime Minister. It read: 'It's a plop. Truman.' A new, glaring light was shed on the future of the war against Japan.[8]

Yet during these pleasant, seemingly so carefree days, nagging thoughts about the Election results persisted; at times Winston was buoyant and confident, while at others he was convinced he was beaten. Clementine was philosophical but on the whole pessimistic, and the rest of us could only, like him, hazard guesses coloured by our own hopes and moods.

On the morning of 15 July the party broke up; my mother, who was nursing a cracked toe and had much to do at home, returned to England. Donning my uniform once more I accompanied my father as his ADC as he set out for Berlin by air for the Potsdam Conference, which ironically bore the code-name 'Terminal'. Half-way through the course of the Conference the British delegation returned to London to receive the results of the General Election, which were declared on 26 July. The dramatic landslide which gave the Labour Party a majority of 146 seats over all parties took everybody by surprise. Clement Attlee, the new Prime Minister, had reckoned even in his most sanguine moments that although the Conservatives would win, they might have a majority of only some forty seats![9]

The Election result was a body blow to Winston. Although on and off in the weeks succeeding Polling Day he had envisaged the possibility of defeat, optimism had on the whole prevailed. The cheering crowds which had hailed him on his Election tours, his enormous standing as a world figure, the expressions of love and enthusiasm his presence had recently evoked in France, combined with encouraging noises from most of those in his close circle of friends and party colleagues, had tended to make him confident of victory.

He himself has described how in the early hours of 26 July, 'Just before dawn I woke with a sharp stab of almost physical pain. A hitherto subconscious conviction that we were beaten broke forth and dominated my mind.'[10] Nevertheless, the overwhelming avalanche of the defeat of his leadership and his party had a stunning effect, and his feelings of hurt and humiliation were intense. Those who loved or served him fell mute, and felt helpless before the spectacle of this fall from a pinnacle of power not often attained by one man in the annals of war or peace.

Those who have neither experienced nor witnessed it cannot imagine the void which opens under the feet of a politician removed from power – either by the will of his political supremo, or by the command of the ballot box. It is part of the price to be paid by those who choose this particular vocation, where the prizes seem so bright, and where the forfeits wound or even destroy, but nevertheless it is a curious and sobering set of circumstances to watch.

Everything is done with great politeness but complete implacability. The Minister's Private Office will perform the 'last rites'; the letter of resignation to the Prime Minister will be prepared and conveyed – or, in the case of the Premier, the Private Secretary will arrange with the Palace for the Sovereign to receive in audience his First Minister to accept his resignation. The flow of the famous red or black boxes is at once diverted, and the special key delicately requested from the former Minister's keychain; the scrambler telephones disappear from his home in the twinkling of an eye; and usually an official car (probably not his own one, which is already in waiting upon his successor) will take this 'non-person' back to his home.

Where an official house is involved matters are usually arranged with mutual courtesy and consideration between the in-comer and the out-goer, but the office is vacated within hours; the business of the State must proceed on its course unruffled.

At any level of Government these procedures are painful – accompanied as they usually are by varying degrees of mortification, disappointment or anger (possibly all three) – but the higher the cliff of power, the more sensational the fall will be.

> He nothing common did nor mean
> Upon that memorable scene.

This quotation from Marvell's 'Horatian Ode' was one which Winston would often recite, and certainly his own and Clementine's demeanour in defeat was admirable. She, indeed, was philosophical. 'It may be a blessing in disguise,' she said. To which Winston retorted: 'If so, it is very well disguised.'

My sister Sarah described those first days after the Election so well:

My mother was out of Downing Street quicker than lightning. She was quite an old hand at this sort of thing and when an election took place while we were occupying a Government house, she was always fully prepared for any result and, if adverse, immediate departure.

They took a suite in Claridges for the time being, until they could find a London house, and I remember him standing on the pavement waiting for his car to arrive to take him to some event or other, and singing gaily to the doorman the old Tivoli music-hall song:

> I've been to the North Pole,
> I've been to the South Pole,
> The East Pole, the West Pole,
> And every other kind of Pole,
> And now I'm fairly up the Pole,
> Since I got the sack
> From the Hotel Metropole.[11]

Winston and Clementine had in fact acquired a house only a few months before – 28 Hyde Park Gate, in Kensington, which was to be their London home for the next twenty years – but it was not yet ready for habitation. Chartwell was still shrouded in dust sheets and needed some alterations, so Clementine had many tasks with which to grapple. Perhaps in this, although she herself was strained and tired, she was the more fortunate of the two;

for Winston, bereft of office and – temporarily – of occupation, there was a dismal void.

It was thirty years since the Muse of Painting had discovered Winston Churchill wandering forlornly in the garden at Hoe Farm; and since then she had proved a faithful and delightful companion. Now she would prove the distracting and healing powers of her friendship once again. It was decided in family conclave that while Clementine wrestled with the two houses Winston would be better out of the way, and a long painting holiday was prescribed.

At this point Field Marshal Alexander (then Supreme Allied Commander for the Mediterranean) offered Winston the use of his villa, La Rosa, on the shores of Lake Como; it had been his headquarters in the last days of the war. This handsome offer was accepted with gratitude, and on 2 September Winston was wafted in the Field Marshal's Dakota aircraft to Italy, accompanied by Sarah (on leave from the WAAF), Lord Moran, a secretary, a detective, and the ubiquitous Sawyers. The next day Winston wrote to Clementine, describing their abode:

My darling Clemmie,

This is really one of the most pleasant and delectable places I have ever struck. It is a small palace almost entirely constructed of marble inside. It abuts on the lake with bathing steps reached by a lift. It is of course completely modernized, and must have been finished just before the War, by one of Mussolini's rich *commerçants* who has fled, whither it is not known . . . Every conceivable arrangement has been made for our pleasure and convenience. Sarah and I have magnificent rooms covering a whole floor, with large marble baths and floods of hot and cold water . . . the weather is delightful, being bright and warm with cool breezes. Yesterday we motored over the mountains to Lake Lugano, where I found quite a good subject for a picture. I made a good beginning and hope to go back there tomorrow, missing one day. I have spotted another place for this afternoon. These lakeshore subjects run a great risk of degenerating into 'chocolate box', even if successfully executed.[12]

He painted a charming lakeside scene of Como, which now belongs to the National Trust, and hangs in the drawing room at Chartwell. To this dictated letter, he added in his own hand:

I have been thinking a lot about you. I do hope you will not let the

52. *Scene on Lake Como, September 1945.* Collection: The National Trust, Chartwell

work of moving in to these 2 houses wear you down. Please take plenty of rest.

With fondest love.

Your devoted husband

W[13]

They were indeed splendidly installed, and Winston's large marble bathroom did double duty as a studio. To make sure all the arrangements were perfect, and also for company, Field Marshal Alexander had ordained that two young officers – John Ogier and Tim Rogers, both from Winston's old regiment the 4th Hussars – should act as his ADCs; it was a thoughtful gesture. Winston warmed instantly to these gallant young men who had 'done' the war, and Sarah described how 'Night after night Charles [Moran] and I would sit back while the boys fought the battles from Omdurman to Alamein.'[14]

Sarah was the best of correspondents, keeping her mother and all of us at home supplied with the holidayers' news. Her first letter recalled that it was the anniversary of the declaration of war:

Just six years ago today . . . I wish you were here with us. I was so distressed to see you so unhappy and tired when we left and so was he. We never see a lovely sight that he doesn't say 'I wish your mother were here.'

The days are filled with painting and picnics. The first picture was a success – a luminous lake and boats backed by a beetling crag, with a miniature toy village caught in the sunlight at its foot . . . The weather is perfect . . . We shall be very happy here. Now at last one can sit in the sun without the thought of war sitting beside one.[15]

As he had in France, Winston drew much attention among the local population, and the whole party was somewhat astonished by the reception the vanquished accorded the leader of their erstwhile foe:

War to them is obviously like everything else in their lives, something physical, a physical catastrophe that happens, is unpleasant, is over and forgotten, like an earthquake, not a moral or an emotional upheaval to be pondered on or a bitter lesson from which something must be learnt. Oh no, the tooth has stopped aching, the sun is shining again. Who won it? Who lost it? Who cares? That was last week, this is today. Look Churchill, Churchill, Viva, viva. Both the young and the old know him. I was astonished at a bunch of children, the eldest not more than twelve, who looked at us calmly and the eldest said 'Churchill'. They can't do enough for us, they bring out chairs to us

142

to sit on, towels to dry our hands with and then retire about twenty yards and sit and watch for hours. Our ADC, I fear, thinks we are too polite. In front of a barrage of smiles it is difficult to be other than cordial . . .[16]

Presently their host, the Field Marshal, came to visit them, staying two nights. Alexander also was a painter, so he and Winston had many things other than past campaigns to talk about, and they spent pleasant hours painting together. Alexander recalled:

> It was a tremendous business when he painted. First there was an enormous easel, the sort that portrait painters have in their studios. Then there was a small table with whisky and cigars. Then there were the paints. He loved colours, and used far too many. That's why his paintings are so crude. He couldn't resist using all the colours on his palette.

Churchill had 'no illusion' about his paintings, Alexander added.

> He once said to me: 'Now don't go out and imagine you are going to paint a masterpiece, because you won't. Go out and paint for the fun and enjoyment of it.' That was what he did.[17]

Although the Field Marshal judged Churchill's paintings 'crude', Sarah found their styles very similar; on 8 September she wrote to her mother about them:

Darling Mummie,

Time flies too quickly, we have already been here a week. He is looking tremendously well and is much happier with every lovely picture and they are really lovely. Care slips away, we've had no newspapers or letters for five days, he was completely resigned about the newspapers, not so about the letters. Thank goodness Alex arrived and brought a lovely one from you. Alex can only stay one day which is very sad but long enough to do one lovely picture. They painted the same scene. It is amazing how their styles are very similar and the painting conversation has been a delight. It roughly goes like this, Alex: 'I always use just a touch of Rose Madder, do you use Rose Madder, Winston?' – 'But of course, I always use Rose Madder, what about Yellow Ochre?' Alex: 'Yes, yes I'm very fond of Yellow Ochre, Yellow Ochre pale is very useful. I tell you what I really like, one shouldn't use it but I always like a touch of pure black on the palette.' Winston: 'Ah now there I disagree with you, no black, Neutral Tint perhaps, but never black. Do you know Neutral Tint? You don't? My dear Alex you must try Neutral Tint, much better than black. I don't like the sepulchral finality of black. I must say I like bright colours.' And so on and so on. Last night I heard them wandering around the house theoretically touching up the positively frightful pictures there and Papa saying, 'Now come here, Alex, come here, now really look at this, we really paint better than the bastard who painted this one.' I really think he is over it, it is hard to tell, but he said last night: 'Every day I stay here without news, without worry I realize more and more that it may very well be what your mother said, a blessing in disguise. The war is over, it is won and they have lifted the hideous aftermath from my shoulders. I am what I never thought I would be until I reached my grave "sans soucis et sans regrets".' The only thing he misses is you . . .[18]

Sarah later recorded more about those pictures which had so drawn the derisive criticism of Winston and Alex:

There were, indeed, some perfectly frightful pictures in the house, and one above all he sat and stared at every evening. It was of a stagnant murky pool and reflected some funereal shubbery. Two sombre fir trees blotted out much of the sky which looked reminiscent of a London fog, and peering biliously between the trees was a pale and sickly sun. That picture became the butt and focus of Alex and my father the evening they were together. After Alex had left, Papa was sitting staring as usual at the offending picture, when suddenly turning to us he said: 'We are all agreed, are we not, that this is the worst picture that has ever been painted?' We murmured assent. 'It takes the palm, the prize for bad pictures; you must say it's offensive?' Again we nodded our assent. In a twinkling of an eye the picture was off the wall, was prised out of its frame and was being carried triumphantly up to the bathroom, which was being used as a studio, to be doctored. Charles groaned: 'He oughtn't to do it, he oughtn't to do it.' 'Oughtn't he?' I asked. 'No,' said Charles, 'but you won't stop him,' and taking up the banner of passive resistance, went off to bed.

I leapt upstairs where my father was squeezing great daubs of vivid colour. The two boys sat on the edge of the bath goggle-eyed. I delivered my lecture: 'You really mustn't,' I said. As the first vivid red hit the gloomy canvas my voice trailed away, suddenly beautiful flaming azaleas appeared on the dingy shrubbery, the dingy firs were given back the new green of their youth, the pallid sun instead of trying to break through the fog with fitful gleam sank in a splurge of glory, and the fog as if by magic disappeared, and the happiest of blue skies smiled down on the whole scene which had been caught by the hitherto stagnant, repellent pool, now a kaleidoscope of reflections. It was breathtaking, it was enchanting, it was lovely. The whole thing accomplished and back in its frame and back on the wall inside half an hour, we sat and admired it for two hours, exhausted but satisfied by this act of 'artistic rape' as my father called it.

Early next morning, one by one we tiptoed down to have a look. What would the morning light reveal? Well do you know, it was still lovely, it glowed brazenly like a bird of paradise and we were all heart-broken when it was once more carried upstairs to have its face washed. It now hangs back on the wall, stagnant and gloomy as before.[19]

Clementine had been overjoyed to hear Winston's good news from his holiday haunt and weighed in with some sage advice: 'I was so much pleased to get your telegram saying that you had achieved some victories in the field of painting,' she wrote on 7 September. 'What Fun! Please don't impose on them but leave them well alone!'[20]

I too had evidence of how serene and occupied my father was during this time; he wrote to me with loving wishes for my twenty-third birthday and added:

> Here it is sunshine & calm. I paint all day & every day & have banished care & disillusionment to the shades. Alex came & painted too. He is vy good. Monsieur Montag is coming to comment & guide me in a few days. I have 3 nice pictures so far, & am now off to seek for another . . .[21]

Charles Montag was the Swiss painting friend from many years ago, who had given Winston so much good advice and escorted him round Paris art galleries. He it was who had arranged for one 'Charles Morin' to exhibit his work for the first time. Now Montag was living in Paris and was the Swiss representative on the Fine Arts Commission. He was a most welcome visitor, and stayed for four days. After he had left, Winston wrote to Clementine:

> He was most helpful in his comments. I do not entirely agree with his style, and when he paints himself it is disappointing, but he has a vast knowledge and one cannot paint in his presence without learning. I am quite embarrassed by the magnificent outfit of colours and brushes which he brought with him. They must have cost him £50 at least, and he is not at all a rich man . . .[22]

This generous gift of artists' materials would indeed have been welcome for, along with much else, such things were in short supply in England at the time.

This most necessary and successful of holidays was now drawing to its end. They had been in that delectable haven for eighteen days; now Lord Moran had to return to his other patients, and Sarah's leave from her unit was nearly expired. Winston, however, was feeling so much freed from cares and so much in his painting stride that he concocted – through the courtesy of higher authorities and together with his military ADCs, who were now the firmest of friends and best of companions – an enjoyable prolongation of sunshine days. He, the two officers, his detective and Sawyers would drive by easy stages along the Italian and French Rivieras, stopping off to paint at propitious places and eventually flying home towards the end of the month. Writing to tell Clementine of this change of plan, Winston described with glee the prospect of an impromptu adventure:

> Tim [Rogers] will scout ahead of us on each stage of our journey and find a sleeping place. We shall come along behind, and stop at any scene that catches my fancy. My party is now very small . . . We are all men, so it will not be difficult for us to fend for ourselves along the route . . .[23]

He also told Clementine that he was sending nine completed paintings back with Sarah:

> . . . I hope you will be able to keep them in their packet till I come, for I am so much looking forward to showing them to you and Mary one by one myself. If of course you cannot bear it, I shall forgive you. I am sure you will consider they are a great advance, particularly the later ones. I am confident that with a few more months of regular practice I shall be able to paint far better than I have ever painted before. This new interest is very necessary in my life . . .[24]

Winston and his companions left the Villa Rosa and lovely Lake Como, where they had spent such a pleasant and restorative interlude, and set out on their tour. Their first stop was at Villa Pirelli, east of Genoa; described by Winston as 'half a marbled palace and half a Swiss chalet', it stood on a rocky cliff overlooking the sea. He told Clementine how here he

> got a beautiful clear water of the palest green to try and paint. I worked hard for two days at the illusion of transparency and you shall judge when you see how far I have succeeded . . .[25]

It was near here that the only disagreeable incident of the whole holiday occurred. At Recco, roving around for a subject to paint Winston decided upon a bombed railway viaduct and houses. At first the usual crowd of small boys appeared and was successfully kept at a distance by his detective, Sergeant Davies. Then gradually the crowd grew larger, and people started to shake their fists and boo. It was not certain whether they actually recognized their unwelcome visitor, but they certainly did not appreciate his painting their bombed homes. Winston at once packed up and drove home to the villa, considerably upset by the incident. He readily admitted that he had behaved somewhat tactlessly, and 'said he would have been damned annoyed if Hitler started to paint the bomb damage in London'.[26]

Crossing the border Winston spent the next ten days or so revisiting haunts that had pleased him in the days before the war: Monte Carlo (where he could not resist a sortie to the Casino!) and Antibes, where he stayed in a villa put at his disposal by General Eisenhower. At Cap Martin he visited the olive grove he had once painted at La Dragonnière. This house now belonged to a relation of Lord Rothermere, whose small children 'who are very nice came out and brought the picture which I had painted eight years ago', Winston wrote to Clementine, adding with triumph, 'It is not a patch on what I can do now, although, as you know, I have hardly touched a brush in the interval . . .'[27]

During the last stages of his holiday Winston's interest in world affairs began to revive. On receiving a batch of British newspapers he described to Clementine how he was 'wading through them', and commented on various items of news which had caught his attention. 'There will be no lack of topic to discuss when we all come together again,' he wrote, adding a sentence or two which revealed how much his holiday had revived him:

> Meanwhile this rest and change of interest is doing me no end of good and I never sleep now in the middle of the day. Even when the nights are no longer than 5, 6, or 7 hours, I do not seem to require it. This shows more than anything else what a load has been lifted off my shoulders.[28]

Winston finally flew back to London in the first week of October; he had painted fifteen pictures during twenty-five days of sunshine. Those weeks of beautiful and changing scenes, of balmy air and good companionship, had restored him in body, mind and spirit. They had distanced the humiliation he had suffered, and put it in proportion. They had afforded him a physical rest he sorely needed after the stupendous and long-drawn-out trial of the war years; and it is right to remind ourselves that he was now in his seventy-first year. But above all he had re-established his 'brush skill', and discovered again his passion for painting.

CHAPTER NINE

Back in London Winston was once more ready to enter the lists. During his absence Clementine had organized the move into their new London house, and Chartwell was more or less habitable again.

Outwardly undaunted by the magnitude of his electoral defeat, Churchill took up his role as Leader of the Opposition, and with his colleagues set about reviving the shattered morale and fortunes of the Conservative Party.

While abroad Winston had spent many hours reading the bound copies of his wartime minutes and telegrams, and already he saw in them the main source for his war memoirs, but for the moment he started to work again on the *History of the English-Speaking Peoples* which had been interrupted by the outbreak of the war.

Like millions of others, Churchill was remaking his life; for him it was a case of picking up the threads of former activities laid aside for a while. As in the thirties his three main occupations were now party politics, writing and painting. As in the thirties he was out of office – but not now as a voice crying in the wilderness to whom too many closed their ears. Although he might nurse the hidden wound of his defeat, his stature and fame were now worldwide; even out of office he wielded influence with his own political opponents and foreign governments. Despite his rejection at the polls, he was held in love and admiration by the greater number of his compatriots of all parties as the 'man who won the war'; while abroad, especially in the former occupied countries of Europe, he was hailed with near adulation as their liberator, and as one whose voice alone had kept hope alive in the long night of their thralldom.

Wherever he went people sought to do him honour and give him pleasure; when he was abroad his hosts would try whenever possible to offer him opportunities for painting, even within an official programme. During these post-election years Churchill travelled a good deal (always, of course, with due regard to the times and seasons of Parliament), both to fulfil official engagements and for consultations. Prime ministers and presidents seemed always ready to learn his views, and to confide in him their hopes and anxieties.

In November 1945 Winston was in Paris, staying at the British Embassy with Duff Cooper (the first British Ambassador to be appointed to France since the Liberation) and Lady Diana. The Coopers were long-time friends who had shared Churchill's fight against appeasement; Duff Cooper had resigned from the Chamberlain Government in protest after the Munich Agreement. There are witty and illuminating vignettes of Winston (or 'Duckling' as she calls him) in letters Lady Diana wrote to Conrad Russell during this visit:

12 November 1945
Early morning. Duckling [Winston Churchill] arrived at 5 yesterday – a picture of cherubic curves and glowing health – with boiler suit discarded in favour of civvies. He looked less porcine – in fact near elegant . . . I was relying on his taking a snooze between tea and dinner and finally forced him to, tho' he says since he has no more work he never sleeps in the day. What a constitution!

Paris 13 November 1945
The Duckling days are in full swing – after writing yesterday we waddled off to the Lou-ver – the director had it opened and a lot of rather undistinguished friends joined in the *cortège*. Duckling, very smileless and silent, stared for a long time at the *Victory of Samothrace*, while M. Salle, the director, told us where and how it had stood and the colours it was painted. From there we passed through the *Salle d'Apollon*, where there is newly exhibited most beautiful *objets d'art*, in gold and lapis and crystal and diamond. These didn't tickle Duckling at all (I must go back and spend an hour feasting my eyes) but he revelled in the pictures, touching their surfaces gently, with his delicate hand. I've never seen pictures stroked before. M. Salle says the Chinese do it. The Chinese wear their nails long so as to appear to be unable to work, but they stroke and finger little jade balls to keep their touch sensitive.

At lunch we had M. et Mme [Lèon] Blum and M. [François] Charles-Roux of the Institute and the afternoon was spent listening to Winston make speeches in his atrocious French to different *academies* in the Institute. He was enthroned in a 'chair' in one of them.

D.[1]

In the first week of 1946 Winston and Clementine with their usual entourage embarked on the *Queen Elizabeth*; they were to spend nearly three months in the United States. Lord Moran had recommended that Winston was better out of England during the bleakest months, for the threat of pneumonia always lurked. Just before leaving Chartwell Winston dictated a memorandum of instructions to Robert Southon, the local builder, about a number of matters he wished attended to in his absence. Among these was a 'painting platform' which was being constructed for use in the Studio.

> The castors for the painting platform are absolutely essential to its use. It is a great burden to me pushing it to and fro across the floor. I trust the castors will be available before my return in March. It is essential that they should work in every direction . . .[2]

In America Winston was able to enjoy sunshine and painting, and to renew his contacts with President Truman. He also undertook several public engagements, including an official visit to Cuba, and culminating in what came to be known as one of his most famous and prophetic speeches – the 'Iron Curtain' speech – at Westminster College, Fulton, Missouri.

In the New Year's Honours List, Winston had been awarded the Order of Merit – an honour of great and rare distinction. Still away in the army I wrote to congratulate him, but my letter shows that despite the fact that his life was again full of work and challenge, there remained the shadow and hurt of his defeat:

> I hope with all my heart you will find a measure of peace and contentment there [in the US] and in this new year.
>
> I can guess at a small part of your sense of disillusion and frustration in these times which to so many seem the dawn of better times and again to so many the twilight of prestige and greatness and unity.
>
> To all who love you – and there are so great a number – it is a grief to see you so set aside – and so saddened. The grief is the greater for the little we can do to help you.
>
> We can only tell you of our unfaltering faith, and burning gratitude and tender love.
>
> From your proud and ever loving daughter
>
> Mary[3]

Winston and Clementine's first destination was Miami Beach, where they stayed with a wartime Canadian friend, Colonel Frank Clarke. My mother kept me in touch with their news, writing to me on 18 January 1946:

> My Beloved Mary,
>
> We arrived here 48 hours ago in tropical heat, rather much, but delicious. And lo and behold in the same night it changed and we are shivering among rustling palm trees and grey skies.

Papa has not yet settled down to painting, and is a little sad and restless, poor darling. I hope is he going to begin writing something.

Later in the day. The weather has slightly improved and Papa has started a picture of palms reflecting in water. I visited him, and draped a knitted Afghan round his shoulders as he was sitting under a gloomy pine tree in a particularly chilly spot.[4]

Indeed, Winston contracted a chill, and four days later my mother wrote to me again:

Papa, thank God, has recovered or nearly so. We had a wretched 36 hours when we telephoned to Lord Moran & the temperature, tho' not very high, simply would not go down & poor Papa was very nervous about himself, & yet very obstinate & would either take no remedies at all or several conflicting ones at the same time.

But today he bathed! & loved it. The weather is now perfect but tropical. Crickets chirp all night – there are lovely flowering hedges and hibiscus pink, lemon & apricot . . . The sea is heavenly – water about 70°.

Papa has learnt a new card game 'Gin Rummy' & plays all day & all night in bed & out of bed. He has started 2 not very good pictures.

Tender love (I must fly Papa is calling) . . .[5]

While Winston and Clementine were in Miami they drove over to visit their old friends Jacques and Consuelo Balsan, who had given up their French homes and now lived entirely in the United States. They had what my mother described as 'a palace in the middle of a jungle',[6] Casa Alva, Lantana, in Florida, where they had recreated the luxurious and civilized life which had always characterized their homes. My mother wrote:

There is a Norwegian Butler, flocks of pale blue parlour-maids, delicious food, ancient French panelling and Aubusson carpets, with a faint feeling of '*ennui*' pervading the whole . . .[7]

It all must have brought back echoes from their many visits to the Balsans in France; but the war years in England had made this elegant life and its setting seem unreal and out of touch.

During the summer of 1946 Winston and Clementine formed a new and much-to-be-valued friendship with Oswald Birley, the celebrated portrait painter, and his wife Rhoda; it seemed to recall the memory of the warm relationship they had enjoyed with the Laverys so many years before. Birley had been commissioned by the Speaker of the House of Commons to paint Churchill's portrait for his Residence in the Palace of Westminster. The sittings were planned to take place in the Studio at Chartwell, but the relationship between sitter and painter got off to a rather sticky start because Winston became awkward and did not want to be distracted from his own ploys. My mother was in London, busy with various engagements, and I was deputed to look after Captain Birley and 'organize' my father and the sittings. There is a rather fussed entry in my diary for 14 June 1946: 'I have spent today chasing Papa to sit for Mr B. – entertaining Mr B. and cooking . . .' Of course I lacked both my mother's status and her courage – eventually, however, the sittings started. Oswald Birley's quiet charm and my father's respect for an artist soon melted away any difficulties, and I was able to leave them to it. On my return from a day in London, I recorded with relief: 'Found Mr B and Papa well-pleased with each other and the portrait.' And the following day: 'Papa sat goodly all day.'[8]

During the course of the sittings Winston and Oswald Birley found many subjects to discuss. Painting was an obvious bond; then there were their shared experiences of the First World War. Birley was a retired captain and a holder of the Military Cross, and valour was always a passport to Winston's esteem and affection. Soon the enchanting Rhoda Birley was invited too; she also became a great friend and in future days would be a perfect companion for Clementine on expeditions abroad. Captain Birley reminded Winston of yet another link between them: he had been one of those judges back in 1925 who had awarded Winston first prize in an amateur painting competition. Moreover, Winston had never claimed his prize – a picture by Oswald Birley, who now suggested that he should paint for him a portrait of his youngest daughter. Everyone was delighted – not least myself, for I had fallen beneath the gentle spell of this charming man. My mother gave the portrait many years later to my husband Christopher, and I am sitting beneath it now as I write.

Later in that summer of 1946 'neutral' Switzerland showed Winston Churchill where her heart lay. A group of Swiss individuals, warmly supported by the federal and cantonal governments, offered him a delightful house on the shores of Lac Léman – the Villa Choisi – for a holiday in August. The house belonged to a Swiss banker, M. Alfred Kern. Winston and Clementine accepted gratefully, and their family was able to enjoy with them the beauties and pleasures of this part of Switzerland. Winston could paint in complete privacy within the villa's grounds, or rove in search of subjects further afield.

Nothing was too much trouble for his Swiss benefactors. When the weather deteriorated General Guisan, who had been Commander-in-Chief of the Swiss army during the war, lent Churchill his campaign tent, which became a perfect shelter within which to paint or write. Winston was now

WSC painting at the Villa Choisi in 1946. The Broadwater Collection, Churchill College Cambridge. Courtesy of Winston S. Churchill, MP. Peter Lofts Photography.

launching into the writing of his war memoirs, and even from his holiday retreat he was contacting former colleagues to verify facts. In one such letter, to Field Marshal Alanbrooke, he gives a glimpse of Swiss lakeside life:

> We have horrible weather here . . . indeed they say it has never been so bad at this season. However, the villa is very comfortable. I have been playing at 'still life' and experimenting in *Tempera* which is a most amusing medium for preliminary work.[9]

Winston had always been open to new ideas and new methods of painting, and the passage of years had not quenched his eagerness to learn. After he returned home he wrote of his new 'discovery' in a letter to Mr Willy Sax of Zurich, from whom in the post-war years he procured many of his paints:

> I have been amusing myself with painting in Tempera, which I find a most delightful medium offering great possibilities both in the ground-work and the finish of pictures, and working in so happily with oil colours in the final stages. I should be much obliged if you could send me in a letter the exact description of the glycerine which you said could be spread upon the colours on the palette to prevent their drying up, and thus avoid needless waste.[10]

Another experiment Winston made at this time was that of working on very large canvases (28 × 36 in. or 40 × 50 in.). These new artistic departures were noted by me in my diary:

> Papa is attacking bigger & yet vaster canvases. He has launched out on one in tempera! He is lost in concentration for hours and hours. At dinner he said: 'I've always had my toys – I've never grown-up – & all my life I've played with toys'. At dinner we drank *'Aux grandes toiles'*.[11]

My father's dalliance with tempera was to prove fickle, although he toyed with it on and off in years to come; he soon reverted, too, to the size of canvas with which he seemed to be most at home (20 × 34 in. or 25 × 30 in.). In my view some of the pictures he painted during this period were not among his most successful; the expression 'picture postcard' could with some justice be applied to many of them. My mother ever encouraged him to use softer and more subtle colourings, and not to 'overwork' his compositions.

Despite the middling weather, this lakeside family holiday was among the most agreeable I can remember. Earlier that year I had been demobilized from the army, and was revelling in civilian life. My sister Diana and her husband Duncan were with us, and also Charles Montag, who had taken a large share in the orchestration of this lovely holiday: his oft-repeated watchwords were *'Tout est prévu'* and *'J'arrange tout'* – which indeed he did. A few special visitors added to everyone's pleasure; Diana Cooper and her son John Julius were staying in the neighbourhood, and Field Marshal Smuts came and stayed for several days. Winston and he spent hours closeted together; my father always set store by this great man's wisdom. Their relationship dated from 1906, when Smuts had been sent over by the Boers to represent their case to the new Liberal Government, in which Churchill was a junior minister at the Colonial Office.

One afternoon my parents gave a tea party for the kind benefactors who had made it all possible – their generosity included lending priceless pictures and bibelots to furbish up the almost fairy-tale villa. Such functions were never my father's forte, however, as my diary recounts: 'Papa loathes tea parties – but waddled in & was amiable . . .'[12] He presented Mme Kern with a still life of melon, peaches and grapes on a silver dish against a background of green velvet, painted on one of the wet days.

At the end of his time in Switzerland Winston visited Lausanne, Geneva, Berne and Zurich. We had been warned that the stoic Swiss were not given to effusive shows of approval or emotion, but in all these cities Winston Churchill was met not only with every conceivable mark of official honour, but also with wildly cheering crowds which thronged the streets and squares. Most unfortunately my poor mother could not accompany him, for a few days before our departure from Choisi she had fallen heavily while on a boating expedition and broken some ribs. In considerable pain she was escorted back to London ahead of Winston. And so it fell to me to be with my father during these unforgettable days.

The weeks at peaceful Choisi had given Winston time not only to paint, and to write his war memoirs, but also to contemplate the larger part of Europe still dazed and ravaged by the war, and to give form to his thoughts and beliefs as to how those countries should turn their backs on past hatreds and together seek a better way ahead.

And it was in a speech to the students of Zurich University on 19 September 1946 that he made his clarion call for prostrated Europe to arise, heal her wounds, and march towards a united future. All this sounds unexceptional now, but at the time his words were regarded in many quarters as forging ahead too fast. This applied especially to his injunction to France and Germany:

> The first step in this recreation of the European family must be a partnership between France and Germany. In this way only can France recover the moral leadership of Europe. There can be no revival of Europe without a spiritually great France and a spiritually great Germany.[13]

In November of 1945 Winston Churchill had been received rapturously by the Belgian people in Brussels, Antwerp and Liège, during the course of his official visit. Now, shortly after his return from Switzerland and in response to a private invitation from Prince Charles, Count of Flanders, the Regent of Belgium, Winston went for a few days of pleasure and painting as his guest. I went with him, for my mother was still nursing her broken ribs. We spent an agreeable day at Dinant, where Winston, on a huge canvas, painted the wide sweep of the Meuse. The next day in Bruges, Winston settled himself in the garden of the Béguinage, a convent, where he was 'attended upon by charming Benedictine nuns';[14] his picture shows some of them walking among the trees reading their missals. Not to be outdone, the local bishop also appeared to pay his respects. Meanwhile, the rest of the party went for a lightning sightseeing tour of some of the fabled treasures of the beautiful and ancient city.

Early in the New Year of 1947 Randolph's son Winston, aged six, received a present and a long explanatory letter from his Churchill grandfather:

Darling Winston,

Thank you so much for your charming card. I now send you a box of very lovely paints, and some brushes. These paints must only be squeezed out a drop at a time, not more than the size of a pea. You can mix them with water freely, using plenty of water; but they dry and become no good any more in about half an hour. You may use about three times as much of the white tubes; that is to say a blob about equal to three peas, each time you paint a picture.

Do not waste these paints for they are very hard to get and come from abroad.

After you have tried them by yourself I hope you will come down here one afternoon so that I can show you myself how to use them.

With much love,

Your affectionate grandfather,

WSC[15]

PS, You do not need to squeeze out all the colours at once, only two or three at a time as you need them.

It has to be recorded that, although the young Winston has grown up to have great abilities, painting is not yet to be perceived among them – but time is on his side.

This year Churchill was to achieve a goal he could certainly never have imagined: the President of the Royal Academy, Sir Alfred Munnings, suggested that he should enter some of his paintings for hanging in the Royal Academy's Summer Exhibition. Winston took some persuading, but finally agreed to the proposition, with the absolute proviso that the pictures should be submitted to the Selection Committee under a pseudonym. Sir Edward Marsh, who had been his Private Secretary in his early ministerial days and was a lifelong friend who often stayed at Chartwell, helped Winston to choose the paintings he should submit. Eddie Marsh was an excellent judge, being an acknowledged art connoisseur. He reported that Winston was himself 'very choosey and resolute'[16] in his judgements. The pictures selected were *Winter sunshine* (p. 58) (the 1925 prize-winner), and *The Loup River, Alpes-Maritimes* (p. 116), painted in the thirties. These were duly sent in under the name of David Winter; only when they had been accepted was the committee given the artist's real name.

The following year three paintings of Churchill's (the maximum allowed 'on the line' by a non-member) were accepted for the Royal Academy Exhibition, and this time he submitted them under his own name. A little while later he was accorded an honour he greatly prized: the Royal Academy elected him an Honorary Academician Extraordinary – a unique distinction.

Sir Alfred Munnings had of course been forward in all these matters, and although he was never an intimate friend, he used to meet Winston on various occasions, including congenial dinners at the Other Club.* Munnings was a flamboyant – not to say rumbustious – character, and prone to ill-considered outbursts. At the Academy Dinner in 1949, in his Presidential speech, he implicated Churchill in an abusive attack he chose to make on 'modern art' in general, and various celebrated modern artists in particular. Winston was much displeased, as this extract from a letter to Sir Alfred shows:

> I . . . heard with surprise your statement that we were walking up the street together when I spoke to you about kicking Picasso if we met him. I do not think we have ever walked up a street together, and any-how this is not the sort of statement that should be attributed to me.
>
> I know you speak on the impulse of the moment, but I protest none-the-less against these utterances.[17]

Winston minded very much that such statements should be attributed to him – they would have been quite out of character, for he was both modest about his own work and respectful of that of others, whether famous or obscure, and whether he admired it or not.

That winter of 1947 Winston spent Christmas in his favoured Marrakech.† It was his fourth visit, and the last time he had been there was in January 1944, after his serious illness. Since 1945 Clementine's health had not been good: the war years, when she had braced herself to carry on with her own considerable burden of war work as well as with the unremitting task of running two households, and all else that falls to a Prime Minister's wife, had taken their toll. This winter found her somewhat exhausted and so, as Sarah was free to go with her father for both care and company, Clementine decided to stay behind at Chartwell. Early in 1947 I had married Christopher Soames, and we were living in the farmhouse in the valley below the gardens at Chartwell. Soon after the war, Winston had bought the farm adjoining Chartwell, and Christopher, newly invalided out of the army, was managing the farm for him. So my mother was not solitary, but spent Christmas cosily with us.

Clementine was somewhat ambivalent about Marrakech as a suitable

---

* This dining club, which always meets at the Savoy Hotel in London during parliamentary sessions, was founded by Churchill and F. E. Smith in 1911. Its members include politicians (of all shades of opinion), writers, artists and lawyers.

† On all these foreign visits during the post-war years when British subjects were financially restricted by draconian currency regulations, Churchill, with his party, was the guest of his publishers, Time-Life International, and the *New York Times*. No breach of the British currency regulations was involved.

winter-holiday place for Winston – although she agreed with his doctors that he should flee the fogs and chills of English winters. She knew from experience how treacherous the North African climate is; the days are brilliant and warm, but out of the sunshine the air bites. Winston and Sarah had departed with her earnest injunctions ringing in their ears, that he must take care not to paint after the evening chill had descended.

We at home were amply supplied with news from Marrakech, for both Winston and Sarah were excellent and frequent letter-writers. They stayed, as Winston had done in the 1930s, at the Mamounia Hotel, and the party (apart from the usual essential back-up of two secretaries, a valet and a detective) consisted of Winston himself, Sarah ('the Mule' as her father affectionately but not inappropriately called her) and Bill Deakin. As a brilliant young Oxford don Bill had worked with Winston during the thirties on the life of Marlborough, and he had then become a firm friend of us all. He had had a brave and brilliant war: as a member of Special Operations Executive he had led the first British Military Mission to Tito in 1943, for which he was awarded the DSO and the Yugoslav Partisan Star. Now he was helping Winston once more – this time with his war memoirs.

Winston wrote his second letter home to Clementine on 18 December 1947:

> We have been here a week today. The weather is lovely and increasingly warm . . . At 10 o'clock in the morning it is possible to lie in bed, as I am doing now, with the French windows wide open on to the balcony. I have been working very hard, rather too hard, in fact. My routine is: Wake about 8 a.m., work at Book till 12.30, lunch at one, paint from 2.30 till 5, when it is cold and dusk, sleep from 6 p.m. till 7.30, dine at 8, Oklahoma* with the Mule – who was given a credit of £28 and has been completely stripped (I have given her another credit, but she says she will not accept it). At 10 or 11 p.m. again work on Book. Here I have been rather naughty; the hours of going to bed have been one o'clock, two, three, three, three, two, but an immense amount has been done and Book II is practically finished. I am not going to sit up so late in the future.
>
> The painting has not gone badly but I only have these two and a half short hours of good light. Three daubs are on the way.[18]

A day or two before, Sarah had written to her mother:

> So far he has not left the hotel, he paints from a high balcony of the new wing of the hotel – and as it has till now been cold, I am glad. But

---

* Another American card game, even more exciting than gin rummy.

today a sortie has been planned – just a small one – to the pink walls. He is inclined to work a little too late. Bill is an enormous help to him – but also a temptation to work on too late at night.

Bill planned to leave Dec 22nd and meet his wife in Paris for Christmas but now great telegrams have been sent to persuade her to come out here for five days so that Bill can stay longer . . .[19]

'Pussy' Deakin duly flew out to join them, and greatly added to everyone's enjoyment over Christmas.

On Christmas Eve, Winston wrote again:

The weather continues to be cloudless and lovely. The air is cold, and in the shade or when the sun goes down it is biting. I am very careful to wrap up warmly and never paint after 5 o'clock. I have five (six now) pictures on the stocks. They are really much better, easier, looser, and more accomplished than those I painted twelve years ago (which I also have with me). I think you will be interested in them. They look much more like the real thing, though none as yet are finished, and there is many a slip.

Yesterday we went for a picnic at Ouriki, where we had three picnics together in 1943/44. Do you remember it? It is an opening of a beautiful gorge in the hills, with great snowy mountains in front and red buildings on either side of the enclosing foothills, and quite a river flowing out of the mountain chain. The whole party went, and I think everybody enjoyed themselves. We are going again in two or three days to the same place so I can finish my picture . . .

I continue to be extremely fit, and my existence is strictly divided into sleeping, eating, painting and the Book with a nightly game of Oklahoma with the Mule . . .[20]

Although Winston painted most of the time as the holiday progressed, corrected proofs were sent back almost daily for the printer. In the same letter, he gave Clementine a report on the book:

The progress I have made is immense. Book I is practically finished and so is Book II. I believe they will cease to be burdens on me except for minor corrections by the end of the year. It would have been quite impossible for me to do this work if I had not buried myself here, where evey prospect pleases, and only the twenty-four hours are too short . . .[21]

Christmas was very festive and merry at the Mamounia, the whole party dining together – Winston joining in the dancing afterwards, and staying up till two o'clock. Loving messages were exchanged with the quieter (but equally happy) party at Chartwell Farm.

Despite all warnings and his own prudent intentions, Winston did stay out painting too late in the afternoons: the result was a cold which persisted and developed into bronchitis. Nervous lest his old enemy pneumonia should be lurking, Winston asked Lord Moran to come out, and to bring his wife with him. Clementine decided to join him too, and she flew out with the Morans on 2 January. The world press got very excited at the idea that Winston might be really ill, and on 4 January he received three British journalists to allay public anxiety. That afternoon he resumed his painting – being careful to come in early. On 19 January the family returned home.

CHAPTER TEN

Back in England Winston plunged once more into politics. *Life* magazine in the United States began to serialize the first part of his war memoirs in April 1948; the *Daily Telegraph* serialization on this side of the Atlantic followed a few months later. The first volume of the memoirs was published in both Britain and America later the same year, to be received with wide acclaim. Meanwhile Churchill pressed forward with the later volumes.

A very old warrior friend, General Sir Ian Hamilton, hailing from India and Boer War days, had died in the winter of 1947. He and Winston had always kept in touch; indeed the Hamiltons had bought the Churchills' house and farm at Lullenden in 1919. In the thirties Sir Ian had supplied Winston with a small stock of Belted Galloway cattle, which he bred, to graze the meadows in the valley at Chartwell. They were, of course, totally unsuited to these lush southern pastures, being essentially designed for survival in their wild native Galloway. Winston was nevertheless greatly attached to them, and particularly admired the way the snowy cummerbund around their pitch-black torsos was perfectly and instantly repeated in the newest-born calf. Eventually the 'belties', as Winston called them, were sold for economic reasons, largely at the insistence of Christopher, who was managing the farm, to be replaced by a more profitable breed. Winston was regretful, writing to Clementine in his 'Chartwell Bulletin': 'I am sorry to let them go as they are most ornamental and characteristic. But there is no doubt that six or seven milch cows of good quality would save three or four hundred pounds a year of loss.'[1]

In his will Sir Ian left Winston a temple figure of a black Buddha seated in a cross-legged position. When in early May 1948 Jock Colville came to stay with Christopher and me at Chartwell Farm, we all visited the 'big house' for dinner one night, and Jock recorded in his diary[2] that Winston had been busy all day painting the Buddha, in front of which he had placed a flame hippeastrum flower in a silver goblet (p. 163). Very sadly the brooding figure of the Buddha, which had a prominent place in the drawing room at

Chartwell before one of the great looking glasses, does not survive; during some spring-cleaning operation it was shattered into a thousand bits. But its handsome portrait bears witness to a long friendship, and hangs now in the front hall at Chartwell.

Painting made agreeable links with some of the Churchills' neighbours – in particular with the Astor family at Hever Castle, about six miles away down the valley from Chartwell. Colonel John Astor* was himself a gifted painter; he had started with watercolours in about 1925, and his great painting companion was his stepdaughter, Lady Margaret Mercer-Nairne (later Myddelton). Presently she switched to oils, and encouraged her stepfather to do likewise. Colonel John and his wife Lady Violet were always most hospitable to Winston and Clementine and their elder children, and during the twenties and thirties Winston quite often painted at Hever, where there is a famous colonnaded Italian garden as well as beautiful lakeside scenes.

At times, however, as the thirties rolled on, relations between the families were a little cooled, for Colonel Astor was chief proprietor of *The Times* newspaper, whose editorial policy was largely supportive of Baldwin and Chamberlain. Some years later, in a letter which he dictated but never sent, Churchill brooded on the attitude *The Times* had taken over various public issues: 'Time after time they have thrown their immense weight on the wrong side . . . *The Times*, apart from personal courtesies, has been a heartbreak to me and a dire oppression to all the ideas for which I stand.'[3] Painting nevertheless proved a lasting bond, and in 1937 Winston wrote a charming letter to John Astor, accompanying the present of a painting table:

> These tables are made by a little man in Norfolk whom Lavery put me in touch with. They have the convenience that they can be easily carried in the one hand with everything inside, including if necessary three wet paintings. It can be used for water colours equally and the attachment with the elastic is intended for this purpose. I have added a small selection of paints and brushes so that you can start on the first Sunday that the grouse allow.[4]

Margaret Myddelton has happy memories of times at Chartwell, writing to me:

> I loved knowing your father as an enchanting *père de famille* . . . and shall always treasure a memory of playing the schoolroom piano (very badly) to accompany him singing 'Oh! My darling Clementine', 'John Brown's body' etc. The singing was energetic, like everything else he did.[5]

---

* Created first Baron Astor of Hever, 1956

53. *Buddha and scarlet hippeastrum, Chartwell, May 1948.* The buddha was bequeathed to WSC in 1947 by his old friend General Sir Ian Hamilton: '. . . the black buddha seated in a cross-legged position [was] taken by Gurkha orderlies and myself from a deserted temple near Mandalay during the Burmese war.' Collection: The National Trust, Chartwell

She also recalled

> a day at Hever when John & I went to look at your father painting in the Italian garden. He had his painting table all laid out before him, a large umbrella over his head & his valet to hand him the extras, such as cigars, brandy, oil etc. He said 'This canvas is a battlefield & I'm going to win the battle'. John was very much impressed, especially because his own approach was such a diffident one . . .[6]

One evening after the war, Winston had a chance to see Colonel Astor's pictures, and he wrote with genuine appreciation:

> Thank you so much for such a very pleasant and interesting evening, which I hope will be productive of good results to our harassed and hobbled country.
>
> I was greatly impressed with your pictures, which show accomplishment and technique carrying them altogether out of the amateur field in which I disport myself. The only comment I would venture to make with great diffidence is that you might try in the near future, just as an experiment, a more brilliant and intense colorization with sharper contrasts and greater depth. This might amuse you as a variant upon your very clearly-marked style.
>
> I also thought that the portraits were very good. I wish indeed I had your facility; though I have strong views my technique is faulty . . .[7]

Winston went on to try to persuade his friend to exhibit his work privately and anonymously 'because I think you would find it rather amusing winning public approbation anonymously'; in the event John Astor was too diffident to act on the suggestion. The letter ends on a political note:

> The times ahead of us are serious, and the issue at the next Election, if not forestalled by graver events, may be decisive upon the British survival as a great power by the side of the United States.
>
> Pray give my regards to Violet. Clemmie hopes to come over and see her very soon.[8]

The summer of 1948 saw one of the most tense periods of the Cold War, for this was the time of the Berlin Blockade. From 24 June the Soviet occupation forces in East Germany had closed all road and rail access to and from Berlin, and from the end of July 1948 to the end of September 1949 the Allies mounted an amazing operation – the Berlin Airlift – to supply 2,500,000 Berliners with every necessity of life. East and West glared at each other, and the situation was as fraught and potentially deadly as it had been at any time since the end of the war. Despite these dark and menacing clouds, I remember a particularly pleasant and harmonious holiday in August 1948, when my parents installed themselves for nearly a month at the Hôtel du Roy René in Aix-en-Provence, and took Christopher and me with them. The evening before our departure from England we dined at Chartwell. I wrote in my diary: 'We drank to *"Nos vacances"*. But the news from Berlin & from Moscow is frightening . . . I wonder if I shall live to set out on a holiday which is not overshadowed by some impending world disaster?'[9]

Aix-en-Provence is the principal town of a region rich in beautiful, interesting and curious sites, affording almost a surfeit of 'paintatious' places – Les Calanques, near Cassis on the coast, Les Baux, and St Rémy with its wonderful Roman triumphal arch, to name but a few. One expedition we made stands out in my memory – our visit to La Fontaine de Vaucluse. The place is historically and romantically associated with the fourteenth-century poet Petrarch, who lived there and languished for love of his Laura, to whom he wrote such beautiful poetry. But people have always flocked to see the *Fontaine*. From the base of a limestone cliff a river wells up from subterranean depths. *La Source* is sinister and secretive, but in a hundred yards a river has rushed into its stride, and the swiftly flowing water is ice-cold, aquamarine and crystal clear. My father, always fascinated by water, found the swiftly changing character of this 'instant' river most compelling, both as a wondrous natural curiosity and as a subject for his brush; he was to come here several times to paint the *Source* and the river in its changing moods.

On this first visit Winston settled himself down by the riverside to paint, supervised by his detective, Sergeant Davies, while the chauffeur and Winston's valet, Greenshields, began spreading out the luncheon. Christopher tied string round the necks of the bottles of white wine and hung them in the glacial river to keep cool; then he, my mother and I wandered off to visit the village. During the course of the day the Mayor appeared and offered a bouquet to Clementine. We lunched long and agreeably by the river, and the afternoon drifted by most pleasantly; we returned home in the gloaming 'sun-soaked & happy'.[10] My father painted a most lovely picture that day of the limpid water in many shades of emerald and aquamarine; my mother later gave the picture to Christopher, and now it is a reminder to me of that perfect summer's day we all spent together (p. 166).

Randolph came out to join us, and presently Bill Deakin – always a welcome addition to our group – arrived to help Winston with his work, which occupied a good slice of every day, and sometimes of the night as well. Walter Graebner, an agreeable American who acted as 'link man' between Winston and Time-Life, came bearing corrected proofs with commentaries from various people. Graebner often visited my father, wherever he

54. *The river at La Fontaine de Vaucluse, August–September 1948.*
Collection: The Lady Soames, DBE

happened to be working, at home or abroad, during the years of the 'war memoirs', and he later wrote a charming book of reminiscences. He recounted a rather touching story from this holiday:

I remember a remark he [Winston] made at dinner once in Aix-en-Provence after a long, happy afternoon in the Cezanne country painting Mont St. Victoire. Deep in thought for several minutes, he suddenly broke into the conversation around him, and said rather gravely:

'I have had a wonderful life, full of many achievements. Every ambition I've ever had has been fulfilled save one.'

'Oh, dear me, what is that?' said Mrs Churchill.

'I am not a great painter,' he said, looking slowly around the table. For a few seconds the embarrassment was so complete that no one could bring himself to say anything, and then the party talked of other things.[11]

Winston was certainly quite sincere in what he said – he would greatly have loved to add this achievement to his curriculum vitae. Perhaps painting was the only alternative profession to politics he would ever have contemplated.

Winston was very possessive of his pictures, although he deprecatingly called them 'my little daubs', and so it was a real sign of gratitude or affection when he parted with one. In spite of his reluctance, he did give away well over a hundred pictures. There is an amusing story of how the painter James Sinton Sleator, a pupil of Orpen, and presently to become President of the Royal Hibernian Academy, came to Chartwell, probably in the twenties, to paint with Winston (at Orpen's suggestion). Professor Thomas Bodkin recounted:

His host's artistry had enormously impressed him. But as a shrewd, humorous Ulsterman he took special delight in telling me how, when the time had come for him to leave, Sir Winston had tried to persuade him to accept a fee for his professional assistance. Sleator, who had felt himself to be a privileged guest, refused and was pressed to reconsider his refusal. He thought to give pleasure by saying that he would greatly prefer the present of a picture. Though Sir Winston so hates to part with his work that he might fairly be described as a collector of it, he graciously granted the request. Sleator, a notoriously casual individual and one wholly indifferent to possessions, forgot to take it away with him. But, though he always loathed writing letters, he sent an apologetic one some days later asking that the gift should be forwarded to him. He received a firm reply to the effect that as he had not bothered to take it with him, he could not have cared much for it, and it had better stay where it was.[12]

My father was generous to Christopher and me as we made our home at Chartwell Farm, lending us quite a number of his best paintings: 'Remember,' he would say, 'they're only on loan.' In fact the 'loans' became treasured gifts; each member of the family over the years acquired his or her 'Churchill collection'.

In 1949 Clementine, after a good deal of pleading, extracted from Winston *The Blue Room at Trent* (see p. 105), to be sold at auction in aid of the Young Women's Christian Association, in whose work she had been closely involved during the war. The picture fetched 1,250 guineas, and was bought by a Brazilian gentleman who presented it to the Art Museum at São Paolo. Winston was more than content with the price – it was a far cry from the 115 guineas for which his picture had been sold at the Balmoral charity sale in 1927. Writing at this time to Oswald Birley, he commented: 'The price paid for "The Blue Room" is of course all humbug. It was made up with seventy percent notoriety, twenty percent charity and, I hope ten percent the actual performance.'[13] Be that as it may, Churchill's paintings were now beginning to be known to an increasingly wide audience. Colour reproductions had appeared in *Life* magazine in the United States in January 1946; he had permitted the use of some of his pictures as Christmas cards; and every year now he exhibited up to six paintings in the Royal Academy's Summer Exhibition.

Churchill travelled a good deal in 1949, but not all the journeys included opportunities for painting. He went to Monte Carlo in the New Year to escape the worst of the winter, and then travelled to the United States in March to visit President Truman and address the Massachusetts Institute of Technology. At home his obligations as Leader of the Opposition were onerous and demanded his constant attendance in the House of Commons. His memoirs too were in full spate; Volume IV was now underway. His summer plans revolved around the first meeting of the Council of Europe in Strasbourg in August. Before that he went with Clementine to stay in a hotel on Lake Garda; they stayed there for about a week, and then moved to Lake Carezza, which he found 'much cooler and most paintable scenery'.[14] The paraphernalia which now accompanied Winston on his travels was considerable. Apart from the tables and chairs, his entire office equipment moved bodily, for now he had again to be in constant and immediate touch with political events at home and worldwide. A room for a studio was also necessary, where he could paint on bad-weather days and keep his painting impedimenta, which Walter Graebner itemized as 'about fifteen frames, several dozen canvases, six or eight easels, and three or four powerful lamps'.[15]

At Strasbourg, Churchill made a major speech in French, which had taken even more preparation than usual. He then took a lively part in all the meetings of the next nine days, and before he left he received the Freedom of the City. At this point Clementine flew home, Winston proceeding to Monte Carlo to stay with Max Beaverbrook, whose delightful villa La Capponcina was nearby at Cap d'Ail. Winston had made his first visit here the previous year, and it was to become a favourite haunt of his. Sometimes Max would be there himself, while at other times he would lend the house to Winston. Perched on the rocks above the sea, below the railway and the road and protected by trees, La Capponcina was an oasis of privacy. It had previously belonged to Captain Edward Molyneux, the celebrated couturier, who had sold it to Lord Beaverbrook just before the war. The garden commanded lovely views, and there was a swimming pool, as well as the sea, for bathers. Christopher and I spent many happy days there, keeping Winston company, as did other close friends and members of the family.

Winston was now in his seventy-fifth year. His health was fairly good, although pneumonia was always a winter risk. In 1947 he had been operated on for a hernia, but had made an excellent recovery. His energy was prodigious, but he was going full tilt, at a rate which might well have daunted a younger man. While he was staying with Lord Beaverbrook he suffered a small stroke; the excellent local doctor, Dr Roberts, was quickly in touch with Lord Moran, who flew out, ostentatiously carrying his golf clubs to allay suspicion. For the same reason, Clementine did not come out to be with him, although she kept in constant touch. It was given out that he had a slight chill. He did not return to Strasbourg, as had been planned, for the closing meeting of the Council of Europe; and he cancelled the last lap of his holiday, which was to have been a few days' painting in Switzerland with Charles Montag and Willy Sax. Instead he returned to Chartwell about a week after this tiresome, but thankfully not grave, incident. Winston made a good recovery, and by mid-October he was up to making two major speeches on two consecutive days. But the stroke did leave its mark, however imperceptible, and somewhat undermined his self-confidence.

A place in the sunshine for a winter holiday was soon under consideration and, ever eager for new places, Winston's thoughts now turned to Madeira; a strong inducement being that Bryce Nairn was now there as British Consul. Winston had telegraphed him in November asking for details: 'query warm, paintable, bathable, comfortable, flowery, hotels etc. We are revolving plans. Keep all secret. Should so much like to see you both again.'[16]

All was duly arranged, and after Christmas at Chartwell Winston and Clementine, with Diana, Bill Deakin and the usual faithful team, set sail in the Union Castle liner *Durban Castle* on 29 December; they arrived at Funchal on 2 January. The last time Winston Churchill had set foot in Madeira had been in October 1899, on his way to the South African war.

CHAPTER ELEVEN

The 1945 Parliament had nearly run its five-year course, so a General Election was anticipated in the coming year. Churchill was in sanguine mood politically, and Brendan Bracken, who saw him shortly before his departure from England, wrote to Beaverbrook 'that he ardently hopes to be back in Downing Street at the beginning of the Spring. He says if we lose the election he will promptly retire and spend the rest of his life in enjoying himself!'[1]

Winston and Clementine had intended to stay in Madeira for several weeks, but they had only been there for nine days when the Prime Minister, Clement Attlee, announced the Dissolution of Parliament and gave out 23 February as the date for a General Election. Winston left at once for home by flying boat, while Clementine stayed on to enjoy the sunshine and the company of Bryce and Margaret Nairn. During his short stay in Madeira, Winston had painted the fishing port.

Churchill played his full part in the Election campaign, addressing meetings in various parts of the country as well as in his own constituency. As a family we were strongly represented on the hustings, for Randolph and the two sons-in-law, Duncan Sandys and Christopher Soames, were all candidates for seats. In the event Randolph was the only one to lose his fight. The results brought a narrow win for Labour, whose huge 1945 majority had dropped to six. It was obvious that another election could not be too far off, and Winston decided for the coming spring and summer to stay at home, concentrating on politics and pressing on with his memoirs. Clementine took this breathing space to make one or two short holidays abroad. While she was in Venice in April, Winston wrote to her from Chartwell with all the domestic and family news: 'I have passed a peaceful ten days at the Chart, & plunged deeply into my task of finishing Vol IV . . . I never had a chance to squeeze a tube to any purpose.'[2]

By December, winter sunshine and the prospect of painting beckoned, and Winston decided to go again to Marrakech. He flew out just before

Christmas, taking with him some of his team of literary advisers – for in the fragile political situation he could not know how long he would have to concentrate on his writing. Early in the New Year Clementine and Diana went out to join him. Winston had discovered a new and fascinating place to paint – Tinerhir – which he described to Clementine as 'a sunlight painting paradise'.[3] Getting there involved flying over the Atlas Mountains to the Sahara side, where there is a valley, and great gorges of marble and red stone; but the two-day expedition he and his party had made soon after his arrival had greatly pleased him, and he told Clementine that he would like to go again and take her there.

Soon after Clementine and Diana had arrived this expedition was organized; Walter Graebner and his wife had joined the Churchills and the party consisted of about fourteen people. But the excursion, in a four-engined Skymaster, might have ended in disaster at its outset, as Walter Graebner was to describe:

> There were fourteen people in the plane, including Mrs. Churchill, one of the daughters, Diana, a cousin, a secretary, a valet and the crew. Churchill always smoked on take-offs if he felt like it, but this time as the plane raced down the runway, he decided to take no chances, and tried to ram his burning six-inch cigar into the receptacle on the arm of his chair; when he found that the cigar was too big for the ashtray, he lifted the metal container out of the arm, deposited the cigar in the hole, replaced the container, and settled down for a snooze.
>
> Hardly had the plane left the ground and started the sharp climb over the Atlas when the smell of burning cigar permeated the cabin and a cloud of smoke enveloped Churchill. He was the first to realize that something was wrong and called for the stewardess. Together they discovered the source of the fire, and in a few minutes enough water was poured down the hole to extinguish it. By this time Churchill had become frightened, and was determined to make doubly sure that the fire was really out. Grabbing his steel-pronged walking-stick he proceeded to ram it down the hole and bash the cigar at the bottom. Still not satisfied, he sent for one of the officers of the aircraft and demanded that the cigar be retrieved. When this was done he announced: 'Now we can go over the mountain.'[4]

The small town of Tinerhir and the area around was in French military occupation, but that presented no difficulties, the Military Governor and his officers being both welcoming and attentive. There was a small hotel there, run by the same group as the Mamounia, and the Churchill party pretty well filled it. Winston was delighted with these new painting fields,

55. *The Gorge at Todhra, Morocco, winter 1950–1.* Collection: The National Trust, Chartwell

and worked away 'with feverish energy all day long'.[5] They stayed only a few days in Tinerhir, but Winston painted about twelve pictures, several of which he would complete later in his Chartwell studio.

Picnics were a great feature of these Moroccan visits. The sites were carefully reconnoitred a day or two in advance by Clementine or another member of the party, keeping a keen eye out for good brush subjects. The cavalcade, which, apart from Winston, his family and guests and the painting and picnic impedimenta, would also include attendant detectives and local police, could easily number ten or more cars. Having arrived at the chosen place, Winston took a little time deciding on the exact spot to set up his easel: once he was happily settled, the tables for the picnic would be set up twenty or thirty yards away. Walter Graebner has described delightfully how Winston

> . . . painted busily away with sublime disregard for the bustle going on behind him, everyone, from Mrs Churchill and assorted elderly peers and generals down, pitched in to help the detectives and Norman the valet, get things in readiness, and everyone hopped up and down from the table as often as he pleased to get what he wanted of food and drink. Everyone laughed, everyone was unbraced.[6]

This time in Marrakech Winston made the acquaintance of Jacques Majorelle, who had lived there for thirty years, creating a most beautiful and unusual house and garden; a well-known French painter, he was particularly famous for his pictures of the North African scene. Winston spent an afternoon with him in his studio, and was gripped with interest by his technique, especially by his use of tempera. Soon after his return to England, Winston wrote at length to Willy Sax about his meetings with Majorelle:

> He [Majorelle] had turned entirely to tempera, which he generally uses in the powder form. He certainly had produced remarkably vivid colour effects, which I have never seen surpassed. I have not used tempera lately. There is no doubt that, for skies in Morocco, it is far superior to oils. Pray let me know the recipe which you recommend for making it possible to paint with tempera over oil. I think you told me about it. There is rather a severe chemical wash which, after it has been applied to the oil-painted surface, renders it fit for tempera. Have you got any of this? If so please send me a bottle urgently.
>
> M. Majorelle also showed me a sky of wonderful blue, the intensity of which I have never before seen. I asked him how he got it and he gave me the enclosed description. I got him to come round to my studio at the Mamounia Hotel and he showed me how it worked. He

56. *Mrs Winston Churchill at the launch of HMS Indomitable, 25 March 1940, at Barrow-in-Furness,*
painted in August 1955 from a photograph. Collection: Winston S. Churchill, MP

paints the surface in tempera from tempera powder with as much white as is desired. Thereafter he takes natural cobalt powder (such as is the foundation I think of cobalt oil paint) and blows the powder on with a little bulb spray. The result is to leave a number of fresh particles of great brilliance on the surface and really the colour was wonderful to one's eyes. Do you know anything about this? It would seem to me that you might be very well advised to look at M. Majorelle's paintings which are a manifestation of the power of tempera, the like of which I have never seen.[7]

Although Winston was always eager to receive instruction, advice and criticism from what he called 'real artists', it is clear that quite early on in his painting career his own manner of painting established itself; outside influences, to a greater or lesser extent, joined and informed the mainstream of his own natural style. Discussing 'natural style' in relation to Churchill, Professor Bodkin wrote in 1953:

> There have been masters of the first rank who painted as instinctively as a bird sings and needed little tuition. Corot was one of these.
>
> Sir Winston Churchill himself is another instinctive painter, though one who is always searching for fresh ways and means to produce the desired results . . .[8]

The earliest influence on Churchill was that of John Lavery; subsequently – apart from the few copies he made of masters (notably Sargent) early in his painting career – the pictures where another artist's influence is most immediately apparent are those done under Sickert's direct influence, in the short period of time when they often worked together. Winston had told Sir John Rothenstein how Sickert 'imparted to me all his considered wisdom about painting . . . but I wasn't an apt pupil, for I rejoice in the highest lights and the brightest colours'.[9] Although he could not adopt Sickert's sombre and muted palette, there is no doubt Winston absorbed much from this great artist, particularly with regard to the preparation of canvases, and the handling and laying on of paint. But perhaps the most visibly lasting mark of Sickert's teaching was the use of the 'magic lantern' and of photographs to help in composing and remembering various subjects – methods which Churchill was still using into the forties and fifties.

One of his most striking portraits was the one he made in about 1954 of his beloved Clementine, painted from a photograph taken when she launched the aircraft carrier HMS *Indomitable* at Barrow-in-Furness in March 1940. Winston had always loved the radiant photograph taken of her as she waved the great ship away, and the sketch portrait is full of vitality; it now belongs to their grandson, Winston Churchill.

On this same subject of photography as a handmaid to painting, Fleur Cowles, the artist, gives a most interesting account of a visit she made to Winston's studio at Chartwell in the early fifties, accompanied by the American elder statesman Bernard Baruch, who was one of his closest friends:

Churchill was dressed for comfort in his famous sky-blue siren suit, padding about in gold-initialled, black velvet slippers. I had never realized his complexion was so very white, nor how blue were his eyes.

The studio was long and narrow, lit by windows at the far end. Paints were piled on a narrow refectory table, so neatly they looked unused. A huge globe of the world, the gift of some Americans, was the room's only adornment. It could have been the room of a monk. As we entered we saw two easels standing side by side. On the right hand one was an almost-finished canvas; on the left was a photograph of the same scene, his beloved North Africa, blown up to the same size as his canvas. I was amazed at his candour: few artists I know would admit they copied photographs . . .[10]

Fleur Cowles has also told me in conversation how astonished she was by Winston's openness about the fact that he used photography to help him paint, but – apart from the fact that candour was a key characteristic of his nature – why should he feel furtive about using photographs in this way? Had he not learned to do so from one of the greatest artists of our century?

CHAPTER TWELVE

Their visit to Marrakech in December 1950 was to be Winston and Clementine's last for eight years; and when they returned home to England on 20 January 1951, it was with the knowledge that the coming year would almost certainly see another General Election. The political atmosphere was febrile. Winston, when he wasn't in London for the House of Commons, concentrated his time at Chartwell, pressing on to finish his book. Clementine, whose health was precarious at this time, went off with Bill and Pussy Deakin to Spain for a spring holiday. During the parliamentary Easter recess Winston wrote to her from Chartwell:

> I had a harrying ten days after you left, what with the broadcast, the Privilege case and other trouble in Parliament, and it is pleasant to have ten days at Chartwell . . .[1]

After recounting sundry items of political and domestic news he continued:

> The sun has shone a little in the mornings but it soon clouds over. There has been a frightful lot of rain. Luckily I have plenty to amuse myself with. So far I have not found time to paint. The Book is a gt standby.[2]

All was not toil; Winston was enjoying a new pleasure and interest in the form of horse-racing. My husband Christopher brought this new diversion into his father-in-law's life, and Winston's first acquisition in 1949, Colonist II, a splendid grey horse, was to win many races for his owner, including, in May 1951, the Winston Churchill Stakes. Winston would make many agreeable excursions to the races in the coming years.

Although he and Clementine had a charming London house in Kensington, Winston most enjoyed receiving guests at Chartwell, where he could show them all his 'toys' and inspire them with some of the enthusiasm he had always felt for the place. Only a few people could actually stay in the house, for the post-war alterations to make it more easily 'runnable' had eaten into the visitors' rooms; so the house party could consist only of closest family, perhaps with a Chartwell 'regular' like 'the Prof', Brendan Bracken or Bill Deakin and, among new friends, the Birleys or Field Marshal Montgomery (Monty). But since Chartwell was a scant hour from London it was an easy expedition for others to come for luncheon and tea.

Winston greatly enjoyed conducting his guests on the 'Grand Tour'; he and the less young and active would drive in the demobilized army jeep while the rest of us followed at our own pace. The party would stop while Winston fed the golden orfe in their oil-green pool – with squirming maggots which were regularly delivered for this purpose – and then the flotilla of black swans on the lower lakes. Both of these were favourite subjects for his brush. He would demonstrate the waterworks, whereby the slender trickle of the Chart well was magnified a hundredfold and made to loop the loop, counterfeiting a mountain stream which poured over the great hunks of rock (transported from the Forest of Dean) to fall into the swimming pool, and from there to nourish the lakes in the valley. During Winston's post-war 'territorial expansionist' period, the Tour included the farms, cattle sheds, pigsties, and the market garden, where he would exercise his *droit de seigneur* by plucking a ripe peach.

But the Studio was the focal point of the afternoon. When he and Clementine first came to Chartwell in the early twenties, Winston had earmarked part of a dilapidated range of buildings situated at the bottom of the orchard for a studio. In the mid-thirties he had enlarged it, adding a bay and larger windows. His pictures were arranged on the walls very much like postage stamps in an album, in fixed wooden frames into which the canvases could easily be slotted; others were stacked on the floor, leaning against the walls. Most visitors were quite taken aback by the sheer number of the paintings displayed here, and Winston would take modest pride in pointing out his favourites and his experiments. Sir John Rothenstein was particularly impressed by the 'tidily arranged rows of clean paint tubes',[3] a feature of Churchill's Studio upon which Fleur Cowles also remarked when she visited Chartwell in the early fifties.[4] A considerable reserve of paint tubes was also kept in a mammoth wooden cabinet, which originally contained a superbly generous gift of Havana cigars dating from Winston's official visit to Cuba soon after the war.

For a time after the war, a studio had been installed in the big drawing room in the house, but Winston soon re-established himself in the original Studio, where he would seclude himself for hour upon contented hour. It was a most comfortable and lived-in place, with a roomy old leather armchair; an open fireplace, where a log fire always burned on chilly days; a tray with whisky and soda (and several glasses hospitably arranged for anyone who might drop in); and a telephone – although no one had the temerity lightly to disturb those precious hours.

Among other visitors in the spring of 1951 was Princess Margaret. In her charming letter of thanks she wrote:

> Thank you so much for showing me all your lovely pictures, and all your fascinating treasures of war. I shall always remember it as being one of the pleasantest afternoons I have ever spent anywhere.[5]

In November of the following year another royal guest, Queen Elizabeth the Queen Mother, would also visit Chartwell, writing afterwards that she had found it 'a great treat'[6] to see all his paintings.

Later in May 1951 the American Ambassador, Mr Gifford, brought President Truman's daughter Margaret to Chartwell. She is a charming person, and Winston was particularly glad to welcome her. From his first meeting with her father at the Potsdam Conference in the summer of 1945, he had felt an instant liking and respect for the then-unknown figure in world politics, upon whom the burden of the Presidency and the mantle of Roosevelt had fallen. His respect had grown into true esteem, and the two men had had a frank and friendly relationship ever since. Winston Churchill entrusted Margaret Truman with a picture to give to her father, to whom he wrote:

> This picture was hung in the Academy last year, and is about as presentable as anything I can produce. It shows the beautiful panorama of the Atlas Mountains from Marrakech. This is the view that I persuaded your predecessor to see before he left North Africa after the Casablanca Conference. He was carried to the top of a high tower, and a magnificent sunset was duly in attendance.[7]

In his reply President Truman wrote: 'I shall treasure that picture as long as I live, and it will be one of the most valued possessions I will be able to leave to Margaret when I pass on.'[8]

In the middle of May Clementine underwent a major operation; it was successful, but laid her low for a little while. At the end of July I went with her for a convalescent holiday to Hendaye, of which we had such agreeable memories from our stay there in 1945. Conscious that time for writing might well be running out, Winston was hard at work on the last volumes of his war memoirs. Volume IV, *The Hinge of Fate*, was published in August, and Winston wrote in a letter to Clementine:

> I am virtually re-writing the early chapters of Volume V as I deal with them. They take four or five hours apiece, and there are twenty in

each. You may imagine I have little time for my other cares – the fish, indoors and out-of-doors, the farm . . . Still, I am sleeping a great deal, averaging about nine hours in the twenty-four.[9]

Later in August, Winston left Chartwell for a well-earned holiday. Bringing Christopher with him, he was reunited with a much-restored Clementine and me in Paris, whence we all proceeded by night train to Annecy, in the Haute-Savoie.

Annecy was not a success; it rained without cease and the lake and mountain scenery looked drear and dripping. After a week Winston decided to go to Venice, so we decamped with our impedimenta of over a hundred trunks, suitcases and smaller articles. Winston nearly failed to reach his destination. As the train approached Venice he leant far out of the window to get a better view, and had not his detective, Edmund Murray, pulled him violently backwards, he would have been struck by a concrete pylon carrying overhead wires. His only comment was, 'Anthony Eden nearly got a new job then, didn't he?'

Our whole party stayed on the Lido, then – and still for a little while yet – a fashionable resort, particularly for the glittering crowd of the film festival world. There was a festival in progress while we were there, but Winston and Clementine carried on their own quiet programme, sheltered from intruding photographers and pushy outsiders by Winston's own two detectives and their Italian counterparts. A small bathing tent had been erected for the Churchills' use, near the steps leading from their hotel, the Excelsior-Palace, to the beach; from this Winston would emerge draped Roman-fashion to swim in the sea. With hindsight one trembles to think what the level of pollution was even then, but the sea-bathing which Winston always greatly enjoyed was deliciously warm, and still just possible despite an occasional 'minestrone' effect.

In the afternoons and evenings he would go off by launch to a painting place, while the rest of us wandered in that most bewitching of cities and feasted on the sights. The grandees of Venetian society put themselves out to be agreeable and friendly: balconies were proffered from which to paint, dinner parties given in Winston and Clementine's honour in glorious *palazzi*, and expeditions to the outer islands organized. Despite these pleasurable activities Winston was working hard at last-minute alterations and corrections to Volume V of the memoirs. A former publishers' proofreader, C. C. Wood (Mr 'Literary' Wood, as Winston would ceremoniously call him, to distinguish him from Mr 'Accountant' Wood, who sorted out his financial affairs) was summoned to Venice to read the proofs for misprints and inconsistencies.

57. *Torcello, near Venice, August–September 1951.* Collection: The Lady Soames, DBE

During this visit Winston painted the great staircase of the Doge's Palace, the Colleoni Statue and the Rialto Bridge (his picture of which hangs in the Harcourt Room in the House of Commons). On a sundrenched expedition to the island of Torcello he painted a really lovely picture of a group of pale apricot houses against a misty grey/pastel-blue sky seen across a canal, very '*à la* Nicholson', as my mother would say. She bequeathed it to me, and it is one of my most enjoyed possessions now.

Winston and Clementine were in Venice for about a fortnight, and a week after their return home the General Election was announced for 25 October. This news was received with relief, for the parliamentary situation had become increasingly fraught as the Labour Government lurched along on its majority of six. During the next three weeks Churchill threw himself into a packed programme of speaking all over the country. The Conservatives were elected with a majority of seventeen, and on the evening of 26 October, the King asked Churchill to form a new Administration. At seventy-six years of age, he was Prime Minister again.

CHAPTER THIRTEEN

As Winston Churchill entered upon his second Prime Ministership his general state of health was the source of much discussion. His constitution was undermined. His increasing deafness was a problem both to himself and to others, and his heart had been weakened by the several small strokes he had sustained. But his mental vigour was astonishing, and his capacity for work could shame a much younger man. His amazing physical constitution might be likened to a great citadel which had successfully withstood the attacks of enemies and the ravages of time – which still stood four-square, but bore both visible and invisible marks of its long and valiant history. He would be Prime Minister for three and a half years, during which period he would reach the age of eighty.

From the moment Churchill accepted the King's commission to form a government there was a question mark over how long he would remain as Prime Minister. Hawk-eyed observers in the press and political circles looked for signs of illness, lack of stamina, or decrepitude. The public at large tended to think his continuing in office a splendid *tour de force* – which of course it was – and the rank and file of the Conservative Party in the country were loyal and strong supporters. But within the more sophisticated echelons of the House of Commons, and indeed of the Government itself, there were whisperings about Churchill's leadership from quite soon after the start of his second term. To put it crudely: the Party had heaved itself back to victory on his shoulders, and now some people felt the time was ripe for him to step down, and hand over the leadership to his heir apparent, Anthony Eden. At times Churchill himself entertained such a plan, but he felt he still had work to do – and the strength to do it. He was aware of the existence of a 'Churchill should go' group, but chose for the most part to ignore it. He once remarked in a genial way to a gathering of important Tories (among whom he knew there were those who thought he should go): 'I mean to carry on until either things get much better, or I get much worse.'[1]

One of the changes the years had wrought was that Churchill no longer applied himself as diligently to detail as he had done during the war years: he was content to delegate very largely to his ministers – reserving his strength and thought for the overall strategic concept, and for those areas where he knew he still had unique experience, skill and influence.

The Conservative ministry that made up the Government of 1951–5 was one of outstanding talent, quite apart from the still towering figure of its chief, as Martin Gilbert writes:

> The first six months of Churchill's premiership had confirmed his ability to be a peace-time Prime Minister, and to act effectively at the age of 77. Even if he was sometimes tired, he presided over, and where necessary controlled, four remarkable men – Anthony Eden, R. A. Butler, Oliver Lyttelton and Harold Macmillan – each of whom administered his portfolio with considerable skill . . . So well was the Government working under Churchill's leadership, that by May 1952 all public talk of his early resignation had been put aside.[2]

Moreover, home politics were for a while muted by the sudden death of the King in the early hours of 6 February 1952. Winston was deeply and personally grieved at the loss of his sovereign, whom he greatly esteemed, whom he had served through the dark and turbulent years of the war, and whom he had come to think of as a true friend. The young Queen aroused in him every instinct of chivalry and hope. In his broadcast to the nation on the King's death, Churchill recalled that his youth had been passed 'in the august, unchallenged and tranquil glories of the Victorian era', so that he might well feel 'a thrill invoking, once more, the prayer and the Anthem "God Save the Queen"'.[3]

For the next three and a half years his paints and paintbrushes were little used. Weekends were spent increasingly often at Chequers, which was all geared for entertaining. Christmases were invariably spent there, and the great house would be packed with children, grandchildren and closest kin. Chartwell weekends were quieter. Winston and Clementine usually spent the Easter and Whitsun recesses there, and part of the summer holidays.

Holidays abroad were of course circumscribed now, by both time and practicality. La Capponcina – an easy journey and not too far away – was a perfect haven, and Winston and Clementine went there twice during this second stint in office. Farther flung, more exotic expeditions were attached to journeys undertaken for reasons of state business, as in the New Year of 1953, when Winston visited the United States (as he had done the previous year) to make contact with the President and his advisers. This time there was a new President Elect – but one who was no stranger to Churchill.

58. *Cap d'Ail, Alpes Maritimes, from La Capponcina, September 1952.*
Collection: Royal Academy of Arts, Diploma Work.

General Eisenhower had won the Presidential Election the previous November, and Churchill was eager to meet him in his new role. He had planned to fly, but Lord Moran was against such a long flight, so Winston and his whole party (which included Clementine, Christopher and me, and Jock Colville, who had returned to Number 10 to be Joint Principal Private Secretary) sailed to New York in the *Queen Mary* on 31 December 1952.

His business in New York and Washington completed, Winston headed for a spell in the sunshine. He flew unperturbed through a tremendous storm to Jamaica, where he had been lent a house, Prospect, near Ocho Rios, by Sir Harold and Lady Mitchell.

It was, as always, a holiday which combined work and play. Winston was in the last stages of completing the sixth and final volume of his memoirs, and a slice was also taken out of his holiday by an official visit to the capital city of Kingston, which was tumultuous and moving but naturally quite onerous, and very hot. Back at Prospect all was kindness and comfort, but the weather was marred by grey skies and torrential downpours. At one point Winston confided to Jock Colville that he would 'give £10,000 to be back at Chartwell'.[4] However the sea-bathing was wonderful, from a private beach with sugar-white sand, and fringed with waving palms, and when the sun did shine it was celestial. Winston managed to paint about four pictures in the fortnight. There were some agreeable friends in the neighbourhood: Lord Brownlow, who lived at a most beautiful estate called Roaring River; and Noël Coward, who also had a house nearby, Firefly. Winston and Clementine liked Noël; they had all met years before, with the Edens and the Coopers, and at Maxine Elliott's. Winston greatly enjoyed Coward's songs, which (most amiably) Noël would play for him; 'Mad Dogs and Englishmen' and 'Don't Put Your Daughter on the Stage, Mrs Worthington' were particular favourites. Winston had found his plays and films – *Cavalcade* and, in the war, *In Which We Serve* and *This Happy Breed* – deeply moving. Another bond was painting. Since the early thirties Noël had diverted himself with painting in watercolours, but on one or two visits to Chartwell, Winston had, as Noël would recount, 'lectured me firmly but kindly about painting in oils instead of dabbing away at water-colours'.[5] Noël became completely converted to oils, latterly using them to paint vibrant, colourful Jamaican scenes.

While we were in Jamaica my mother took me and Christopher over to Firefly to see Noël; my father sent messages, but preferred to stay immured at Prospect wielding his brush. We had a lovely time, and Noël recorded in his diary that my mother '. . . appeared genuinely impressed by my banana paintings, and carried a large one away with her, frame and all, to show the Prime Minister'.[6]

186

Winston and Clementine returned from their New Year holiday to a year of unprecedented work and bustle, caused by the approaching Coronation of the Queen in early June. An extra burden of representation and entertaining was laid upon them by the serious illness in May of Anthony Eden, then Foreign Secretary. The year before, he had married Clarissa Churchill, Winston's niece, and now, less than a year later, this cruel illness necessitated his going to America to undergo an operation.

Winston himself was in pretty good health, but a year before Jock Colville had found that 'his periods of lowness grow more frequent and his concentration less good. The bright and sparkling intervals still come, and they are unequalled, but age is beginning to show.'[7] Winston had an amazing capacity to gear himself up for whatever was required, and at his best he was still very good. But everything was achieved by a stupendous effort of will, and it took, inevitably, a toll on his health and strength.

Winston seemed to weather the ceremonies and festivities surrounding the Coronation quite well; but at a great dinner and reception at Number 10, on 23 June, in honour of the Italian Prime Minister, he sustained a stroke at the end of dinner, only minutes after he had made a brilliant impromptu speech. The onset of the stroke was slow, the effects barely perceptible, and the guests departed without its being generally realized that anything was amiss. The next day Winston attended a Cabinet Meeting, and again nothing was suspected. He then drove to Chartwell, but on his arrival he could not get out of the car. During the next few days the paralysis extended down the whole of his left side; Lord Moran feared he might not live. A conference with President Eisenhower and the French Prime Minister had been planned to take place shortly in Bermuda; this was now cancelled, on the grounds that the Prime Minister 'has had no respite for a long time from his very arduous duties and is in need of a complete rest . . .'[8]

Winston remained secluded at Chartwell for a month. The truth about his illness was kept secret from all but a small circle of family and closest colleagues, and during those weeks Churchill made a really astonishing recovery. His strength returned slowly but steadily. On 18 August he presided at his first Cabinet Meeting since he had been taken ill, and on 12 September he attended the St Leger at Doncaster races with the Queen and the Duke of Edinburgh, going on afterwards to stay for two days at Balmoral.

Shortly after this Winston went to stay at La Capponcina, taking Christopher and me with him, to complete his convalescence. Clementine remained at home to have some rest herself: the strain of the last two months on her had been enormous.

187

In the peace and seclusion of La Capponcina, Winston pondered the question which was in the minds of all those 'in the know': could he carry on? This dilemma hung like a cloud over the pleasant sunshine days. At first he found no energy to paint, but he wrote regularly to Clementine 'in his own paw', and the handwriting is remarkably clear and firm. One of his letters is signed 'Ever your loving and as yet unconquered . . . W',[9] with a drawing of one of his 'pigs'.

Winston's health was markedly better, but Christopher noticed that his energy was short-lived and that his 'desire to work – so formidable before – has dwindled to nothing . . .' After five days I wrote sadly in my diary:

Papa is wretched – he is struggling to decide about his future – And altho' when people come to lunch he has been animated and talked well and vigorously – afterwards he has felt torpid, and merely wants to go to bed or read. His paints have been untouched . . . It's inexpressibly poignant to watch him . . .[10]

The very next day, however, Winston sent a triumphant telegraph to Clementine: 'Have at last plunged into a daub . . .'[11]

During this visit Winston hardly left the grounds of La Capponcina, finding plenty of subjects to paint within its bounds. Since 1950 one of Winston's detectives had been Detective-Sergeant Edmund Murray, who would nearly always be on duty during painting holidays, as he was now, for he was an amateur painter himself. Winston liked this very much; he compared painting notes with him, and sometimes asked his advice. Sergeant Murray was also an expert at placing the easel in just the right place, and beautifully setting out all the painting paraphernalia.

When Christopher and I had to return home our places as companions were filled by Jock and Meg Colville, to both of whom Winston was devoted. But it is touching to see how much he missed Clementine: 'I do hope my darling you have found the interlude restful and pleasant. I must admit I have had a good many brown hours . . . I wish you were here for I can't help feeling lonely . . .'[12]

But even in these 'brown' days Winston had been steadily recovering his strength and formulating his decision to carry on. Even on the literary front his mind had begun to contemplate a project for the immediate future: the completion of his *History of the English-Speaking Peoples*. He had laid this aside at the beginning of the war, and it had then been superseded by the war memoirs, the last volume of which was now on the brink of publication. At La Capponcina Winston had been rereading some of the early chapters of the *History* and making plans to set about finishing it.

On his return to England at the end of September, Winston picked up the reins of government without more ado. The first public test of his recovery and ability to carry on was the major speech he had to make at the Conservative Party Conference at Margate on 10 October. It was a formidable ordeal. Apart from the agonized anxieties of those who knew the facts, there were curious questioning eyes and ears, agog to judge the extent of his recovery, for wild rumours had been circulating during these last weeks.

Winston was on his feet for fifty minutes. His concentration and delivery were not to be faulted. It was, as *The Times* put it, 'a triumphant return to public life'. Many years later I was to write of that moment: 'Doctors, closest colleagues, loving relations – all of us had been confounded. As we looked back over the harassments and anxieties of the past months, it seemed miraculous.'[13]

CHAPTER FOURTEEN

In 1953, a dramatic and eventful year both for him personally and for the nation, Winston received two immensely distinguished and glamorous marks of honour. Shortly before her Coronation the Queen created Winston Churchill a Knight of the Garter. King George VI had offered him this ancient accolade (which lies in the personal gift of the sovereign) on his resignation in 1945, but, cut to the quick by the British people's rejection of him, Churchill had begged leave to decline the honour. It is rare to be offered the Garter, rarer still to refuse it, and rarest of all to be offered it again. Winston was deeply moved by the Queen's gesture, and it made him happy to be able to accept this signal honour from the daughter of the sovereign he had held in such high esteem and affection.

Later that year, in October, he was awarded the Nobel Prize for Literature, a distinction which naturally greatly gratified him. With the Prize comes a handsome tax-free sum of money, which was also a source of pleasure; about such agreeable happenings my father was wont to remark, 'A little bit of sugar for the bird.'

An earlier mark of favour by the Queen had been the origin of a new friendship for Winston. In the autumn of 1952 she had commissioned Oscar Nemon to sculpt a bust of her Prime Minister for Windsor Castle. Winston felt greatly honoured, and proud to think that the bust would be in the company of those of his ancestor John, Duke of Marlborough, Nelson and Wellington. During the course of the sittings Winston (together with his whole family) took a great liking to the sculptor. Oscar Nemon was a Yugoslav-Jewish refugee who had made his home in England; he was a man of great charm, gentleness and understanding. His keen sense of humour enabled him to bear with apparent equanimity the annoying vagaries of his sitter. Nemon has since recounted that on one of his several visits to Chequers Winston was making an attempt to sketch him – so he duly posed. Presently he asked if Winston would allow him to see his work, and saw that he had made five or six sketches on small bits of paper. Winston was shy of his efforts, and tore up the drawings; one of them, however, fell on the floor and was rescued from oblivion by Nemon. The drawing is now in the possession of a patron and friend of Oscar's, Mr Bartlett Watt of Toronto, who has kindly allowed me to reproduce it here. As far as I know, it is the only drawing by my father that exists. It is also rather a good likeness of Oscar Nemon.

WSC's pencil sketch of Oscar Nemon, drawn at Chequers, c. 1952.
Collection: Mr F. Bartlett Watt of Toronto

In 1954 Nemon sculpted Churchill again, this time for a statue for the Guildhall in the City of London, which was to be unveiled by the Lord Mayor the following year. Oscar evidently had an inspiring effect on Winston, who suddenly decided he would like to try his own hand at sculpture, and they agreed that they should sculpt each other. Nemon later sent Mr Bartlett Watt an account of his 'duel', as he described it. The two artists had not been at work long

when he [Churchill] became excited about the difficulties in which he found himself. His cigar began to come to pieces in his mouth and soon he was roaring like a lion over its prey. He shouted at me, 'How on earth can I work when you keep moving?' In the interest of continuing peace between us, I kept still after that and, by doing so, lost an opportunity of making a real study of him – a sad loss but almost inevitable because he was a restless and most unwilling sitter.[1]

Thanks to Oscar Nemon's kind and unselfish nature we have the only sculpture ever attempted by Winston Churchill. The unique plaster cast is in the Studio at Chartwell. The head, like the sketch, bears a good resemblance to Nemon. It also represents quite an achievement, as David Coombs, the compiler of the catalogue of Churchill's paintings, attests:

> For a first essay into sculpture at the age of eighty the result is certainly creditable; it is not easy for a painter to have to think and work in three-dimensional form after a forty years' war with flat-bosomed canvas.[2]

Oscar Nemon himself, who later had the head cast in bronze, wrote to the bashful new sculptor: 'I beg you not to underrate the artistic value of this work, which would be considered by any expert as outstanding for a first attempt.'[3] And thirty years later, he would pay a moving tribute to Winston Churchill, whom he had seen in such a special context:

> I knew him well (material for a whole book), he was shy in the presence of men of knowledge and skill, and humility and graciousness in manners was a characteristic of his personality. For that alone he deserves a monument![4]

The highlight of our domestic life in 1954 was my father's eightieth birthday. Of course we, his family, would have celebrated it with joy and triumph, but it turned into an occasion of national rejoicing, for which preparations were in hand months before the actual day, 30 November. The two Houses of Parliament decided to present Winston with his portrait, and commissioned Graham Sutherland to paint it.

The ten sittings were nearly all at Chartwell, and they began in August. Although Winston disliked sitting for his portrait, and artists found him a restless subject, he was always interested to get to know a painter. Fleur Cowles gives an interesting account of an interview she had with Graham Sutherland in 1971. Churchill and Sutherland got on well together, and Winston had demanded at the outset, 'Are you going to paint me as a bulldog or a cherub?' To which the painter replied, 'This depends on what you show me!'[5]

Sutherland actually painted the portrait back in his house in Kent, from studies he made at the sittings. Winston would dearly have liked to have

59. *Portrait head of Oscar Nemon, 1954*: unique plaster cast.
Collection: The National Trust, Chartwell

seen the sketches at the end of each session – a wish the artist firmly, and for the most part skilfully, circumvented despite Winston's wheedling: 'Come on, be a sport, after all I am a fellow painter!' When Winston did glimpse some of the drawings he was full of criticisms and suggestions, which no doubt the painter resisted.

Sutherland seems to have come to like his subject during the long hours of work. He told Fleur Cowles:

He was always considerate, always kind, always amusing and coopera-tive. When he wasn't cooperative, he didn't know he wasn't being cooperative. I think this fair to say . . . He *meant* to be cooperative, and in fact often was. We talked about everything, not only painting, but politics and so on. I think we got on well . . .[6]

Sutherland, looking round Winston's studio, had an interesting com-ment to make about his painting. They had been talking about Sickert, and Sutherland had said to Winston, 'Well, you worked very well with Sickert.' He went on to remark:

that he did better under Sickert than under anyone. As far as art is con-cerned he was very impressionable. If some quite bad painter said he should work in a certain way; in that way he worked. He was very mal-leable in that way; it was a strange sort of modesty . . . He'd take advice from any painter who happened to be there.[7]

Sutherland would return to this point after Churchill's death. Writing to the second Earl of Birkenhead (the son of Winston's great friend and brilliant contemporary, F. E. Smith), who was gathering material for a one-volume life of Churchill,* he observed:

. . . He had extraordinary talent as a painter, particularly when he was not under the influence of some artist or other. But Sickert had a good influence in that, under it, Winston's pictures became less competent and more profound. The painting became more probing, and less an unquestioning acceptance of everything Winston saw before him. His style became much more conceptual.[8]

Graham Sutherland and his charming wife Kathleen, who sometimes came with him, were much liked by both Winston and Clementine, and by the other members of the family, but alas, as is now so well known, the story ended in tears. When Churchill saw the finished portrait, delivered to

* Lord Birkenhead died in 1975 with only part of the book completed. The unfinished work has recently been published (see source notes).

Number 10 about a week before its formal presentation at a great gathering in Westminster Hall, he took a violent dislike to it. Clementine, who had been shown the picture by Graham Sutherland before Winston saw it, had at first sight seemed inclined to like it, but later she came to share Winston's feelings. Seeing how deeply he was upset by the picture she promised him that 'it would never see the light of day'.[9] After the presentation the picture was taken down to Chartwell, where it remained in its crate until it was destroyed on Clementine's instructions, probably in 1955 or 1956. It was not until shortly after my father's death in 1965 that my mother told Christopher and me that the picture had been destroyed, and it was not generally known until after Clementine herself died in 1977, when her executors issued a statement of the facts. But not even private upset over the Sutherland portrait could mar the wonderful birthday celebrations, or dim Winston's deep sense of emotion and gratitude for such a remarkable gesture on the part of his parliamentary colleagues.

The Queen, other members of the royal family, his friends, political colleagues and foes alike and countless numbers of ordinary people joined in celebrating his birthday; telegrams and letters – over 23,000 of them – poured in from all over the world.

During these last months pressure was growing within the Cabinet for Winston to make a firm decision about the date of his retirement. Time was running short now for his successor to establish a new administration before the life of this Parliament expired and another General Election had to take place.

Ever since Stalin's death in 1953, Churchill had cherished the hope that he might be able to make personal contact with his successor, and that the new regime might be encouraged to soften its outlook and policies. In the last years of his power he worked consistently to try to bring about once more a top-level conference of the 'Big Three'; it was a deep disappointment to him that this was not to be.

Churchill still wielded great influence in the United States, and had visited President Eisenhower in June 1954, when the full implications of the power of the hydrogen bomb were being appraised. His realistic understanding of the changed nuclear scene, expressed and developed through the British Chiefs of Staff Paper on Global Strategy, had a distinct impact on American attitudes and policy.

These two large concerns were among the major factors which made Churchill cling to office in those last years. Sir Norman Brook (later Lord Normanbrook), Secretary to the Cabinet, a most wise and charming man who was greatly devoted to Winston but still clear-sighted and detached, later wrote of his Chief as he was at this time:

He could still rise to the great occasion, by an effort of will and a modest use of the stimulants [pills] prescribed by his doctor. But in the daily round of his responsibilities he no longer had the necessary energy, mental or physical, to give to papers or to people the full attention which they deserved.[10]

It was time to go. Clementine had wanted him to retire long before; her heart had never been in this second Prime Ministership. Of course she had soldiered on, in spite of the fact that she herself was feeling the burden of 'life at the top', and since 1953 had been afflicted on and off with neuritis, a painful and wearing condition which persisted for some time. No one understood better than she how hard it was for Winston to make the final decision and give a firm date for his resignation. As she said to me, 'It's the first death – & for him, a death in life.'[11]

Towards the end of February 1955, the date which would (despite some waverings on his part) not now be changed was set for 5 April. This date was not public knowledge when Churchill introduced the Defence White Paper in the House of Commons on 1 March: it was to be his last great parliamentary speech. For three-quarters of an hour he spoke with vigour and brilliance on the perils and agonizing dilemmas presented by the development of the hydrogen bomb. His peroration deserves to survive alongside his great war speeches:

> The day may dawn when fair play, love for one's fellow men, respect for justice and freedom, will enable tormented generations to march forth serene and triumphant from the hideous epoch in which we have to dwell. Meanwhile, never flinch, never weary, never despair.[12]

On the evening of Monday 4 April, the Queen and the Duke of Edinburgh dined at Number 10 together with a distinguished company of guests from Churchill's public and private life, and his closest family. The next day Winston Churchill presided over his last Cabinet Meeting, then drove to Buckingham Palace to tender his resignation to the Queen. The following evening he drove down to Chartwell: 'It's always nice to come home,' he said.[13]

Winston's morale was quite high over the Easter weekend which followed his resignation. Although press comment was limited by the continuing strike in the London newspaper industry, warm and gratifying messages from countless people poured in; and quite a crowd gathered round the gateway at Chartwell to cheer and salute him. Forty-eight hours after laying down his office, Winston started work again on his *History of the English-Speaking Peoples*; and on 12 April he and Clementine, who was suffering acutely from a return of neuritis, flew off for a holiday in Sicily. The paints were packed, and they had tried and trusted companions in 'the Prof' and Jock Colville. Largely owing to cold and rainy weather, however, the holiday proved something of a failure; Clementine's neuritis persisted, and Winston found only indifferent subjects to paint. One canvas survives, a flat and dull painting of the Grotto of the Ropemakers at Syracuse.

On their return two weeks later Jock was nevertheless able to tell Lord Moran that Winston had been in 'good spirits; no regrets; no looking back'[14] and that he had played bezique and painted for hours on end. Winston also reported to Lord Moran how pleased he was to find he still took pleasure in painting: 'I painted with great vigour . . . what mattered was that I found I could concentrate for three hours – I got interested in it, and was always late for luncheon.'[15]

About a month after their return from Sicily, there was a General Election, called by the new Prime Minister, Anthony Eden, to establish his administration. The Conservatives won a solid majority of 59 seats: it was a great tribute to the record of the outgoing Government and to its leader.

Winston had not been invited to take part nationally in the Election campaign, either on platforms or on radio and television; he had, however, been quite active in making speeches in his own constituency and also in support of political neighbours. In Bedford he spoke for Christopher, who was fighting (as it turned out successfully) his third campaign there.

Winston's mood after the Election was particularly benign. He worked busily on his book at Chartwell, and had many letters to answer and to write; he was still very much in the forefront of people's minds.

On 2 June Winston suffered an arterial spasm, which affected his balance and his handwriting for some days. By 8 June, although still rather unsteady, he was well enough to go to the House of Commons and take his seat in the new Parliament, where he was given an emotional welcome from all sides of the House – and from the public galleries. The seat accorded him by the unspoken consent and approval of the whole House was the one he had occupied in the 'wilderness' years leading up to the war – the seat below the gangway, alongside the Treasury Bench. He was to occupy that seat with laudable regularity for nigh on another nine years. (The day after his death in January 1965, from where I sat in the Speaker's Gallery to hear the tributes to my father from the House, I was deeply moved to see that the time-honoured place had been left empty.)

Although Winston made a quick recovery from the spasm, he was deeply afflicted by depression and inertia. He responded to the stimulus of visiting friends, however, and was still able to gear himself up for an occasion, such as going to the Guildhall on 21 June to witness the unveiling of the statue of himself sculpted by Nemon. Work was proceeding on his book with his devoted team of researchers. Among the visitors who saw him at his best was Dr A. L. Rowse, the historian, with whom he had a long and fruitful session.

For some little while Sir John Rothenstein had been of the opinion that an example of Winston Churchill's work should have a place in the Tate Gallery collection. He felt that although it would be 'an acquisition fascinating in the way in which, for instance, a landscape by the Elder Pitt would be . . . the chief consideration was that if one of the very best could be secured, it would be an acquisition worthy in its own right'.[16] The Tate Gallery Trustees were of the same mind, and Sir John accordingly wrote to Churchill, assuring him that they wanted one of his pictures for artistic and not political reasons; moreover, that they had waited until he was no longer Prime Minister before broaching the subject with him.

Winston of course was greatly gratified, and invited Sir John to Chartwell in mid-July 1955, to select a worthy picture. The one eventually chosen was *The Loup River, Alpes Maritimes* (p. 116). It had been painted in 1936, and depicts a bend in the river near the main Cagnes to Grasse road; in Sir John's opinion it 'exemplifies his [Churchill's] unusual perception of light effects over water'.[17]

Sir John has written most interestingly of his various visits to Winston, both in London and, more often, at Chartwell, where he came on several occasions, often to help Winston select his now annual entries for the Royal Academy. Several times Sir John picked out pictures which Winston himself had not rated highly, such as two pictures painted in early 1920 at Roehampton (the home of his cousin Freddie Guest), of cedar trees seen through drifting mist. Rothenstein wrote: 'The two mist-veiled trees had a magical touch, to which he himself, however, seemed entirely unresponsive.'[18]

Sir John Rothenstein also described how, during the many hours Churchill and he spent in the Studio, Winston asked him for 'any criticism of his painting I might care to make'; as he was obviously sincere in his request, Sir John did so, and he gave this account of Winston's reaction:

My first detailed criticism of one of his paintings had an unexpected, indeed a positively startling result . . .

'Oh,' Mr Churchill said, 'I can put that right at once; it would take less than a quarter of an hour,' and he began to look out the appropriate brushes and colours. 'But this painting, surely,' I said, 'must be amongst your earliest.' 'I did it about twenty years ago,' he conceded. 'Well then,' I protested. 'Surely it's impossible for you to recapture the mood in which you painted it, or indeed your whole outlook of those days.' 'You are really persuaded of that,' he grumbled, abandoning the notion of repainting with evident reluctance. This was the first of several occasions when I had to persuade him to desist from repainting an early work in consequence of some criticism of mine. If pride could be exorcized by a single experience (which, alas, being a rank weed it cannot) my own would have been exorcized by the spectacle of 'the greatest human being of our times' prepared to act so confidently upon my advice. 'If it weren't for painting,' Mr. Churchill observed as we left the studio, 'I couldn't live; I couldn't bear the strain of things.'[19]

Finally Sir John made this appraisal of Churchill as a painter:

> He does not paint more ambitious pictures, pictures with complex compositions, peopled by human figures, quite simply because he cannot. But a man is to be measured not so accurately by the impressiveness of his gifts or by his technical efficiency, as by the use he has made of them. Cabanel was a far more skilful painter than the Douanier Rousseau, as is Dame Laura Knight than Mr. L. S. Lowry, yet most lovers of painting would agree that Rousseau and Mr. Lowry are the more considerable artists . . . By the skilful choice of subjects within his range yet to which he can respond strongly he is able to paint pictures of real merit and which bear an intimate and quite direct relation to his outlook on life. In these pictures there comes bubbling irrepressibly up his sheer enjoyment of the simple beauties of nature, water, whether still, bubbling, or agitated by wind; snow immaculate and crisp; trees, dark in their density or dappled by sunlight; fresh flowers and distant mountains, and above all sunlight at its most intense.[20]

It is pleasing now to realize that at this time, despite moments of gloom and inertia, Winston still could and did feel life held interest and pleasure. Sir John records that Winston said to him: 'I look forward to a leisure hour with pleasurable agitation: it's so difficult to choose between writing, reading, painting, bricklaying, and three or four other things I want to do.'[21] I think it was only as old age and increasing feebleness began to take their inevitable toll that my father came to experience boredom; I do not believe that before his eighth decade he would have known how to define the word. O happy man!

On top of the pain of her neuritis, Clementine broke her wrist during that summer, and she went away for a recuperative holiday to St Moritz. Now that she was released from the burdens of official life and the great strain of the last lap at Number 10, her stay in the mountains helped to ease tension and soothe pain, and she returned to Chartwell much restored. In the middle of September she and Winston, taking Christopher and me with them, went to La Capponcina, made available once more by the hospitable and generous Max Beaverbrook.

Over the years that followed, until Winston's travelling days were done, La Capponcina would be a frequent haven. Clementine once wrote to Max of the 'sunshine, the peace & the rest' they looked forward to enjoying there, and told him Winston would say 'there are a 1000 pictures to be painted from Max's garden!'[22] In 1958 they would be there together to celebrate the fifty golden years of their marriage.

This holiday in the autumn of 1955 was a happy one: Christopher and I were company for Clementine while Winston, who was in good health, painted away for hours at a time or reburnished chapters of the *English-Speaking Peoples*. Christopher was also excellent company for him, jollying him along in his grey hours, teasing him affectionately and playing cards with him. Clementine, despite her long dislike of the Riviera, actually stayed a whole month, while Winston, no longer tied so rigidly to the sittings in the House of Commons, remained on until the middle of November. When Christopher and I had to return home, there was a change of guard, and Sarah and Diana went out to be with our parents.

Anthony Montague-Browne was now an important and vital feature in Winston's life, and remained so until Winston's death ten years later. After his war service in the RAF (he was a holder of the DFC) Anthony had entered the Foreign Service, and in 1952 had joined the Private Office at Number 10, quickly gaining the trust and liking of both Winston and Clementine. After Winston's retirement, Anthony Montague-Browne was seconded by the Foreign Office to be his Private Secretary. Churchill was to remain a world figure until the day of his death, and his affairs, both public and private, needed the surveillance of someone experienced in public service. Giving up the prospect of a brilliant Foreign Office career, Anthony devoted himself to Winston. Clementine also relied on his counsel in many matters, and he became, and has remained, a true friend to all our family.

CHAPTER FIFTEEN

In January 1956 Winston made the first of many long visits he would make over the next four years to La Pausa, the French home of Emery Reves. Born in southern Hungary, Reves had made a career for himself as a literary agent; by the time he met Churchill in 1937 and began acting for him, he was handling the syndication of articles by leading political figures in sixty countries. During the war most of Reves's family were murdered; he himself became a British subject in 1940, and was badly injured in a London air raid. Very soon after the war Winston revived his contact with him, and Reves negotiated for him the sale of American rights in his war memoirs. Reves himself acquired the foreign-language rights in the memoirs and the *History of the English-Speaking Peoples*, thereby making a great deal of money for both himself and his client.

Emery Reves lived in the United States, and also had a large and lovely house on the Riviera; La Pausa was near Roquebrune, on the steep hillside above Cap Martin. Emery and the beautiful and lively Wendy Russell (a former New York model a good deal younger than himself), whom he was soon to marry, had together invited Winston and Clementine to stay with them. The invitation was particularly well timed: Clementine's health had deteriorated again that winter and, after a spell of several weeks in hospital in London, she and her great friend and cousin Sylvia Henley were planning to go on a sea voyage to Ceylon. Now, knowing that Winston would be in good hands, and surrounded with care and pleasant company, she could embark without anxiety on her long journey.

From La Pausa there are splendid views towards Menton on one side and Monte Carlo on the other; and Wendy had created a most lovely sea of grey-blue, which lapped up to the terrace of the house, by planting the whole garden with lavender. Winston was to spend many peaceful and contented hours in those lovely grounds.

Not only was La Pausa most comfortable and agreeable to stay in, but Emery and Wendy also had a beautiful collection of pictures, mostly by the

Impressionists. Winston was able to revive the pleasure kindled in him so long ago in Paris, when Charles Montag had opened his eyes to the beauty of the Impressionist masters. As he had done in times past, when staying with Philip Sassoon, Winston tried his hand at copying some of the pictures in the house.

Since his resignation Winston had been seriously considering buying a villa of his own somewhere along the Riviera coast which he liked so much. From La Capponcina he had made several expeditions to look at properties, and during the first few visits to La Pausa, accompanied by Emery and Wendy, he did the same. But the 'dream villa' he sought was not easy to find, and the prices of property on that coast were already beginning to soar. Clementine had always been frankly aghast at the idea; she dreaded the burden of expense and the toil of yet another house to run, particularly as it would be in a part of the world which held little allure for her. More-over, Emery and Wendy were insistent in their offer that Winston and Clementine should stay with them whenever, and for as long as, they liked; gracefully and sincerely they said that Emery owed his fortune to Winston, and it made them happy to make this – indeed handsome – gesture of grati-tude. Gradually, then, the hunt-the-villa game ceased.

Winston was very happy at 'Pausaland', as he called it, and the Reveses were attentive and charming hosts and companions, not only seeing to his every need and wish, but also inviting members of his family out for visits. Clementine went a few times, but she was never really happy there; Win-ston led his own life of painting and cards and writing, and although he wanted her to be there, it must be admitted that he was not much of a com-panion. Emery and Wendy made welcoming gestures, but they and Clementine had little in common, and she found life at the villa claustro-phobic and solitary. So she stayed at home, and as her health improved she found her own ploys, and friends to visit while Winston was away.

Winston's stays at La Pausa were often enlivened by visits from friends who happened likewise to be staying along the coast. One such was Rab Butler* (also a 'Sunday' painter of merit). In 1956 Rab and Winston – polit-ical colleagues for so many years – spent congenial hours painting together in the garden at La Pausa, sitting back to back – Winston painting a seascape with rocks and pines, while Rab painted the mountains behind.[1]

During the next six years Winston spent an average of seventeen weeks each year abroad, seeking the sunshine he so much loved. Perhaps subcon-

---

* Richard Austen Butler (RAB) (1902–82) was the Conservative MP for Saffron Walden 1929–65. He held junior ministerial posts before the war, and was Minister of Education in the Coalition Government; Chan-cellor of Exchequer 1951–55; Lord Privy Seal; Leader of the House of Commons; Home Secretary; Deputy Prime Minister after 1955; created a life peer, Lord Butler of Saffron Walden, 1965.

sciously he also sought to be a little removed from the political life in which he could no longer play a vital part. Many agreeable weeks were passed in 'Pausaland' and there were also more visits to La Capponcina, where Clementine liked to go too. As time went on and he became less mobile, and painting was more of an effort, sea cruises with a friend of his later years, Aristotle Onassis, were a new pleasure. In this unfatiguing, pleasant way, Winston was able to visit far-flung places which would otherwise have been impossible for him. In the course of the eight cruises he made in Onassis's fabulous *Christina V* between 1958 and 1961 (sometimes accompanied by Clementine, and always by a harmonious group of family and friends) Winston floated by Caribbean islands, touching down here and there. He made a marvellous day's visit to Bridgetown in Barbados in 1959, where he was received with enthusiasm in crowded streets; indeed wherever he appeared he was recognized and hailed as a hero by old and young alike. The Mediterranean and her classical islands also offered him sunlit sailing weeks, and it was in *Christina* that Winston made his last visit to the United States in 1961, during the course of a voyage from the Canaries and the West Indies to Palm Beach and New York City.

Back at home Winston led a carefully structured life: he often attended debates in the House of Commons, and he made a few speeches in his constituency. He greatly enjoyed his sorties to the races with Christopher, and was a faithful attender at the convivial dinners of the Other Club. 'Songs' at Harrow School were also a firm fixture in his diary.

The prime ministers who succeeded Churchill were assiduous in keeping him informed of events, and still sought his opinion. In 1957, when Anthony Eden resigned, Churchill was among those sent for by the Queen to give advice as to who should succeed him as Prime Minister. Foreign visitors called upon him – most notably the German Chancellor, Konrad Adenauer, in 1959, with whom Churchill had a lively and useful talk, and later General de Gaulle, who came to see him in 1961 in the course of his State Visit to London.

The years from 1956 to 1958 also saw the completion and publication in four volumes of Churchill's last great work of history and literature, his panoramic *History of the English-Speaking Peoples*. But as the fifties slipped by, time inexorably took its toll on his strength; he suffered another stroke in 1956, and bronchial pneumonia and jaundice in 1958. He also grew deafer, and at times became remote from us all; yet, like a log smouldering in a dying fire, he would suddenly brighten and sparkle, surprising those around him with his comments or questions. Painting remained a pleasure for some time yet, though perhaps he was slower, and the dash and vigour were gone. As he had written, prophetically, nearly forty years before, painting is a friend who makes no undue demands, excites to no exhausting pursuits, keeps faithful pace even with feeble steps, and holds her canvas as a screen between us and the envious eyes of Time or the surly advance of Decrepitude . . .[2]

In the new year of 1958, from far across the world, came a vivid reminder of the scope and talent of Winston Churchill, in the form of a travelling exhibition of some forty of his paintings. The exhibition started in Kansas City on 21 January, and some days later Clementine wrote triumphantly to Winston (at La Pausa): she had read in the *Daily Mail* that '1,221 persons visited your Exhibition in one day at Kansas City and that this is a record'.[3] Subsequently the pictures would be seen in the Metropolitan Museum in New York and in other important cities in the United States and Canada, before travelling to Australia and New Zealand.

Winston had flown from the fogs of winter in England to 'Pausaland' in the middle of January. Feeling an anxiety born of past experience, Clementine wrote to Wendy a few days later to urge that Winston should be persuaded to paint '*before* lunch instead of *after* . . . I'm so afraid of his catching cold when the sun begins to decline at about 3.30.'[4] Wendy duly transmitted the warning and Winston wrote to Clementine:

The sun shines every day and I hope to begin painting *indoors* fairly soon. At present I am dawdling in bed till lunch, but I agree with what you write in yr letter to Wendy that the mornings are the best.[5]

Writing the next day (again in his own hand) Winston gave Clementine a further reassuring report:

My darling Clemmie,
   I have started painting again: *indoors* for the snow is on the hills all round. Flowers arranged by Wendy is the subject & she has painted for three days herself just from memory. It is much better to have a model. The sun shines brightly & today I got up before luncheon and sat in the porch.[6]

In spite of Clementine's concern and Winston's good intentions he was laid low about a month later by a bout of bronchial pneumonia, which at first looked ominous, followed by an attack of jaundice. From both these maladies he recovered, but his health and strength now began to decline slowly but steadily; from now until his death he would need to have a nurse. It was the beginning of a long twilight, illuminated by shafts of sunlight from the glory of the departing day.

After rather a quiet summer Winston had made a fair recovery, and a

60. *Oranges and lemons, 1958.* Collection: The Hon. Mrs Celia Perkins

brilliant shaft of light shone indeed in November, when General de Gaulle (earlier that year elected Leader of a Government of National Safety, and in December to be elected President of the French Republic) invested Winston Churchill with the Croix de la Libération, the highest award reserved for those who had served with the Free French Forces or with the Resistance.

The year in which Winston would attain the age of eighty-five, 1959, was marked by several auspicious events in his diary. Early in the New Year he and Clementine returned after eight years to Marrakech; with him were Jock and Meg* Colville and Biddy Monckton,† who proved a most congenial party. Since Winston's last visit Morocco had gained its independence from France. Jock Colville was later to recall for Martin Gilbert that on the party's arrival

> there was an enormous Guard of Honour provided by the King of Morocco, but Winston, aged 84, pulled himself together, strode down the steps of the airline and inspected the whole Guard of Honour without showing any signs of age or illness.[7]

Winston and Clementine stayed at the Mamounia Hotel, as usual, for about five weeks. The Colvilles and Lady Monckton left after about ten days, and my mother wrote to me:

> The first ten days were enlivened by Jock, Meg and Biddy Monckton – When Papa heard that Biddy was coming without Walter, he was rather sulky . . . But soon he took to her like a house on fire & kissed her tenderly on departure. As for Meg, she & Papa flirted outrageously & almost romped . . . When they all went away poor Papa fell into the doldrums – He is better now & has started a picture from the terrace outside his bed-room. . . . Thank God Papa is blooming in his health. His memory fails a little more day by day & he is getting deafer. But he is well. I have learnt to play poker & enjoy it very much . . .[8]

Although this holiday was such a success, Winston painted only two pictures. He and Clementine left the Mamounia and Marrakech on 17 February; it was to prove their last visit to a place which had given Winston great contentment and pleasure for many years. At Safi two days later they boarded the *Christina* as guests of Ari and Tina Onassis, to cruise along the

---

* Formerly Lady Margaret Egerton, she had married Jock Colville in 1947. Both Winston and Clementine were devoted to her.

† The wife of the first Viscount Monckton of Brenchley who, as Walter Monckton MP, was successively Minister of Labour and National Service and Minister of Defence in 1950s' administrations.

WSC painting on his balcony at the Mamounia Hotel, Marrakech, 1959.
Courtesy of the *Sunday Times*.

Moroccan coast and visit the Canary Islands. It was a joy when, at Tangier, their old friends Margaret and Bryce Nairn (now Consul General there) came on board.

They arrived home on 2 March, and only four days later Winston flew off to stay with Emery and Wendy at La Pausa. During the few days he spent in London he and Clementine went to a private view of the exhibition of his paintings in the Diploma Gallery of the Royal Academy.

Even for professional painters – 'real painters', as Winston would call them – this would be a high-water mark. Winston was rightly and deeply gratified, and his family was infinitely proud. To the paintings which had just completed their world tour were added twenty-six more, chosen for the most part from the Studio at Chartwell.

Sir Charles Wheeler, then President of the Royal Academy, wrote in his preface to the catalogue:

> In his best works Sir Winston reveals not only a skill of hand but, which is much rarer, a selective eye. It is this quality of vision which raises the majority of his exhibits here above any ordinary level . . .

The visitor, on entering the galleries, will immediately become aware of the artist's emotional response to the effects of nature and visual truth, and will be conscious of the enormous satisfaction Sir Winston has received during more than forty years by applying paint to canvas with a bold and joyous brush.

I think it is truly this feeling of his zest for life which is most powerfully conveyed in Winston Churchill's paintings. As I stood in one of the galleries at the exhibition, gazing – amazed anew – at the array of my father's paintings, a woman standing next to me said to her companion, 'What lovely holidays he must have had!'

It was during this spring's visit to La Pausa, when painting was still a ploy and a pleasure for Winston, that an old friend and 'brush' companion from the past appeared again: Paul Maze and his wife came to luncheon at the villa. It must have brought back the memory of their painting side by side in the sunshine at St Georges-Motel in the summer of 1939, only a short space before the dark tide of war engulfed Europe. Winston and Paul made plans to paint together again, but Winston wrote to Clementine that the weather was cold for painting outside, and the painting project had perhaps to be postponed. Clementine must have been relieved that Winston was at last showing some caution about the weather. Her most important news from home was that in the course of thirteen days 38,397 people had been to see the Exhibition at the Royal Academy. 'Your pictures are attracting such big crowds . . .'[9] she wrote proudly.

Back in London in mid-April Winston suffered another slight stroke. Undaunted (and against the advice of specialists) he pressed on determinedly with his engagements. He attended a dinner at the Other Club, where it was noticed that he was not at his best; but at a meeting in his constituency, a week after he had suffered the spasm, he made a speech and managed pretty well. For a little while now, Winston's speeches had been largely written for him by Anthony Montague-Browne, although he himself would carefully peruse and correct the draft. At this meeting Winston announced that he would offer himself as the Conservatives' candidate at the forthcoming General Election; this was received with tumultuous applause.

A visit to the United States was planned, and presented a considerable challenge to Winston. He was determined to go and would not take Lord Moran, as he did not wish to appear an invalid; he was accompanied by Anthony Montague-Browne and his valet-nurse. In Washington he stayed at the White House, where the President, General Eisenhower, was all care and kindness. He saw old friends and colleagues, two of whom, John Foster Dulles and General George Marshall, were even more fragile than himself;

indeed, both of them died during the course of the year. Winston made a short speech or two, and people found him in remarkably good form. Before he left he gave the President one of his pictures, *The Valley of the Ourika and Atlas Mountains*; in his letter of thanks Eisenhower wrote that he had put the picture in his office at the White House, 'so that I may display it proudly to each and every visitor there'.[10] Winston returned to England by way of New York, where he stayed for two days with his old friend Bernard Baruch. We at home were consumed with anxiety, and received him back with joy and intense relief. 'After this stimulating but tiring week in the United States,' I was to write later, 'he returned home safe, if only fairly sound, to England; he had "got away with it" again.'[11]

Winston fought one more electoral battle at Woodford (Essex) in the General Election campaign of 1959: his last. This was the fifteenth campaign Winston and Clementine had fought together; they were now eighty-five and seventy-four respectively. Winston made several speeches in his own constituency, and only one outside its bounds on behalf of a political neighbour. He was returned with a handsome majority, and would remain the Member for Woodford for another five years, until he made his last appearance in the House of Commons just before the 1964 General Election – less than a year before his death.

In the autumn of 1959, a year in which for an old and ailing man Winston had certainly undertaken a goodly ration of engagements, he performed one more task which surely gave him satisfaction. He flew to Cambridge, and planted an oak and a mulberry tree on the site of Churchill College, the scientific institution which was founded by him in 1958, and which bears living witness to how, even in his last years, Winston Churchill could cast his mind forward to the needs of his country in an increasingly technological age.

But now his stamina was failing, and his pace becoming slower. In 1960 he attended the splendid Garter Service at Windsor for the last time. A little while before, he had presented the Queen with one of his pictures for her private collection – the *Palladian Bridge at Wilton* (p. 52), painted in about 1925. The Queen wrote in her own hand to thank him: 'Philip and I are so thrilled to have one of your pictures for our gallery – we do thank you most sincerely for this very kind gesture, and we do appreciate having such a delightful picture with a gloriously peaceful English summer scene. What a truly lovely place Wilton is and you have captured the feeling and pleasure of being there so well that all can feel it too.'[12]

Later that year another of his paintings, *Cork Trees at Mimizan*, was sold at Sotheby's for £7,400, in aid of the World Refugee Fund for which Clementine had made a broadcast appeal. The financial value of his pictures was steadily rising, and would continue to do so.

But now his desire and power to paint were waning; although on a visit to the South of France in September 1960 he had spent some days in the garden at La Capponcina, writing to Max Beaverbrook that he had enjoyed painting there, and sitting in the beautiful sunshine. Soon he would lay down his brush, and be content simply to gaze at the pleasant sunlit prospect.

Over forty years before, Winston had wandered in the garden at Hoe Farm, cast down with misery by the catastrophe of the Dardanelles; 'then it was that the Muse of Painting came to my rescue – out of charity and out of chivalry, because after all she had nothing to do with me . . .'[13]

So now, perhaps, that same kindly Muse who had been his companion for so long saw how it was – and quietly walked away.

Happy are the painters, for they shall not be lonely. Light and colour, peace and hope, will keep them company to the end, or almost to the end of the day.[14]

L'Envoi

When Earth's last picture is painted and the tubes are twisted and dried,
When the oldest colours have faded, and the youngest critic has died,
We shall rest, and, faith, we shall need it – lie down for an aeon or two,
Till the Master of All Good Workmen shall put us to work anew!

And those that were good shall be happy: they shall sit in a golden chair;
They shall splash at a ten-league canvas with brushes of comets' hair;
They shall find real saints to draw from – Magdalene, Peter, and Paul;
They shall work for an age at a sitting and never be tired at all!

And only the Master shall praise us, and only the Master shall blame;
And no one shall work for money, and no one shall work for fame.
But each for the joy of working, and each in his separate star,
Shall draw the Thing as he sees it for the God of Things as They Are!

RUDYARD KIPLING

Notes

The books referred to in the notes are given in the bibliography which follows. For the sake of simplicity, Martin Gilbert's *Winston S. Churchill* and *Companion Volumes* to the biography are given as *Churchill* and *Companion* respectively, followed in each reference by the volume number and, where appropriate, the part number. The following abbreviations have also been used: WSC for Winston Churchill; CSC for Clementine Churchill; and RSC for Randolph Churchill.

CHAPTER ONE

1. WSC, *Painting as a Pastime*, p. 14. Originally an essay, this was first published in two parts in the *Strand Magazine*, in December 1921 and January 1922. It was included in WSC *Thoughts and Adventures* as two separate essays entitled 'Hobbies' and 'Painting as a Pastime', and first published in volume form in 1948.
2. Woods, *A Bibliography of the Works of Sir Winston Churchill*, p. 196
3. WSC, *Painting as a Pastime*, p. 16
4. Ibid. p. 17
5. Lavery, *The Life of a Painter*, p. 177
6. WSC to H.H. Asquith, 11 November 1915. Gilbert, *Companion III: 2*, p. 1249
7. WSC to CSC, 19 November 1915. Spencer-Churchill Papers; Gilbert, *Companion III: 2*, p. 278
8. WSC to CSC, 10 January 1916. Spencer-Churchill Papers; Gilbert, *Companion III: 2*, p. 1366
9. WSC to CSC, 22 January 1916. Spencer-Churchill Papers; Gilbert, *Companion III:2*, p. 1388
10. Quoted in Gilbert, *Churchill III*, pp. 658–9
11. WSC to CSC, 22 February 1916. Spencer-Churchill Papers; Gilbert, *Companion III: 2*, p. 1434
12. WSC to CSC, 28 March 1916. Spencer-Churchill Papers; Gilbert, *Companion III: 2*, p. 1467
13. WSC to CSC, 2 May 1916. Spencer-Churchill Papers; Gilbert, *Companion III: 2*, p. 1498
14. Lavery, *The Life of a Painter*, p. 177
15. Marsh, *A Number of People*, p. 105
16. WSC to CSC, 27 March 1920. Spencer-Churchill Papers; Gilbert, *Companion IV: 2*, pp. 1057–9
17. WSC to CSC, 27 March 1920. Spencer-Churchill Papers; Gilbert, *Companion IV: 2*, p. 1059
18. WSC to CSC, 31 March 1920. Spencer-Churchill Papers; Gilbert, *Companion IV: 2*, p. 1062
19. Gilbert, *Churchill III*, p. 1307
20. Professor Thomas Bodkin, 'Churchill the Artist' in Eade (ed.), *Churchill By His Contemporaries*, p. 290
21. WSC to CSC, 18 August 1922. Spencer-Churchill Papers; Gilbert, *Companion IV: 3*, pp. 1958–9
22. Gilbert, *Churchill IV*, pp. 556–7
23. Undated letter. Lavery, *The Life of a Painter*, pp. 211–12
24. Obituary notice, *The Times*, 5 January 1935
25. Gilbert, *Churchill IV*, p. 894

CHAPTER TWO

1. CSC to WSC, 10 February 1921. Churchill Papers
2. WSC to CSC, 14 February 1921. Spencer-Churchill Papers; Gilbert, *Companion IV: 2*, p. 1352
3. WSC, *Painting as a Pastime*, p. 15
4. Ibid. p. 18
5. Ibid. pp. 18–19
6. Diary entry for 3 July 1953. Moran, *Winston Churchill: The Struggle For Survival 1940–1965*, p. 419
7. WSC, *Painting as a Pastime*, pp. 27–8
8. Ibid. p. 26
9. Gilbert, *Companion V: 1*, p. 895
10. WSC to CSC, 19 September 1921. Spencer-Churchill Papers
11. Ibid.
12. Ibid.
13. WSC, *Painting as a Pastime*, pp. 24–5

CHAPTER THREE

1. Oswald Birley. This account is written in Birley's own hand, on a piece of paper which is stuck to the back of the picture.
2. From the reminiscences of Clementine Churchill. Mary Soames Papers
3. Information about Sickert and his painting is chiefly drawn from Baron, *Sickert*
4. Gilbert, *Companion V: 1*, p. 1048
5. WSC to Lord Stamfordham. Gilbert, *Companion V: 1*, pp. 1052–3
6. Professor Thomas Bodkin, 'Churchill the Artist' in Eade (ed.) *Churchill By His Contemporaries*, p. 291
7. Sir Frederick Ponsonby to WSC. Gilbert, *Companion V: 1*, p. 1052
8. WSC to Lord Stamfordham. Gilbert, *Companion V: 1*, p. 1052
9. Gilbert, *Companion V: 1*, p. 1053
10. WSC to CSC, 26 September 1927. Gilbert, *Companion V: 1*, pp. 1054–5
11. WSC to CSC, 26 September 1927. Gilbert, *Companion V: 1*, pp. 1055–6
12. Gilbert, *Companion V: 1*, pp. 1078–9

CHAPTER FOUR

1. Quoted in Woods, *A Bibliography of the Works of Winston Churchill*, p. 9
2. WSC to CSC, 27 August 1929. Gilbert, *Companion V: 2*, p. 61
3. WSC to CSC, 1 September 1929. Gilbert, *Companion V: 2*, p. 68
4. Ibid.
5. CSC to RSC, 12 January 1932. Randolph Churchill Papers; Gilbert, *Companion V: 2*, p. 393
6. WSC to RSC, 20 January 1932. Randolph Churchill Papers; Gilbert, *Companion V: 2*, p. 394
7. Ibid. p. 396
8. Gilbert, *Churchill V*, pp. 428–30
9. Stanley Baldwin to WSC, 2 May 1932. Gilbert, *Churchill V*, p. 430
10. WSC to Stanley Baldwin, 3 May 1932. Gilbert, *Churchill V*, p. 431
11. Violet Pearman to Nancy Pearn, 20 October 1932. Gilbert, *Churchill V*, p. 441

CHAPTER FIVE

1. Paul Maze to WSC, 13 March 1936. Churchill Papers: 2/252; Gilbert, *Companion V: 3*, pp. 70–1
2. Quoted in Gilbert, *Churchill V*, p. 797
3. Paul Maze to WSC, undated but probably written 13 November 1936. Churchill Papers: 1/268; Gilbert, *Companion V: 3*, p. 411

4. Rothenstein, *Time's Thievish Progress*, p. 129
5. *Dictionary of National Biography*; entry on Nicholson by Eric Newton
6. Ibid.
7. CSC to WSC, 22 August 1934. Spencer-Churchill Papers; Gilbert, *Companion V: 2*, p. 854
8. WSC to CSC, 25 August 1934. Gilbert, *Companion V: 2*, p. 856
9. Steen, *Pier Glass: More Autobiography*, p. 12

CHAPTER SIX

1. WSC, 'Election Memories' in *Thoughts and Adventures*, p. 213
2. Balsan, *The Glitter and the Gold*, p. 217
3. Details of Maxine Elliott's life are taken from Forbes-Robertson, *Maxine*
4. CSC to Sarah Churchill, 14 January 1960. Mary Soames Papers
5. CSC to Mary Soames, 20 March 1951. Mary Soames Papers
6. Forbes-Robertson, *Maxine*, pp. 249–50
7. WSC to CSC, 16 August 1934. Gilbert, *Companion V: 2*, p. 848
8. CSC to WSC, 22 August 1934. Gilbert, *Companion V: 2*, p. 854
9. WSC to CSC, 11 September 1935. Spencer-Churchill Papers; Gilbert, *Companion V: 2*, pp. 1257–8
10. Sheean, *Between the Thunder and the Sun*, p.36
11. Ibid. p. 41
12. Ibid. p. 37
13. Ibid. pp. 32–3
14. WSC unpublished note, 1947. Gilbert, *Churchill V*, p. 686
15. WSC to CSC, 26 December 1935. Spencer-Churchill Papers; Gilbert, *Companion V: 2*, pp. 1163–4
16. WSC to CSC, 30 December 1935. Spencer-Churchill Papers; Gilbert *Companion V: 2*, p. 1365
17. WSC to CSC, 8 January 1936. Spencer-Churchill Papers; Gilbert *Companion V: 3*, p. 11
18. WSC to CSC, 15 January 1936. Spencer-Churchill Papers; Gilbert, *Companion V: 3*, p. 13
19. Ibid.

CHAPTER SEVEN

1. Professor Thomas Bodkin, 'Churchill the Artist' in Eade (ed.), *Churchill By His Contemporaries*, p. 290
2. CSC to WSC, 29 January 1937. Spencer-Churchill Papers; Gilbert *Companion V: 3*, p. 558
3. WSC to CSC, 2 February 1937. Spencer-Churchill Papers; Gilbert, *Companion V: 3*, p. 573
4. WSC to CSC, 5 September 1936. Spencer-Churchill Papers: Gilbert *Companion V: 3*, p. 336
5. Lloyd Papers: Gilbert *Companion V: 3*, p. 336
6. WSC to CSC, 13 September 1936. Spencer-Churchill Papers; Gilbert, *Companion V: 3*, p. 341
7. Quennell, *The Wanton Chase*, p. 108
8. WSC to Dr Thomas Hunt of St Mary's Hospital, Paddington, 28 August 1936. Churchill Papers: 1/235; Gilbert, *Companion V: 3*, p. 331
9. WSC to CSC, 2 February 1937. Spencer-Churchill Papers: Gilbert, *Companion V: 3*, p. 575
10. WSC telegram to Maxine Elliott, 4 September 1937. Churchill Papers: 1/300; Gilbert, *Companion V: 3*, p. 760
11. WSC telegram to Duke of Westminster, 19 September 1937. Churchill Papers: 1/300; Gilbert, *Companion V: 3*, p. 766
12. WSC to CSC, 10 January 1938. Spencer-Churchill Papers; Gilbert, *Companion V: 3*, p. 884
13. WSC to CSC, 18 January 1938. Spencer-Churchill Papers; Gilbert, *Companion V: 3*, p. 891
14. WSC to CSC, 18 January 1939. Churchill Papers: 1/344; Gilbert, *Companion V: 3*, pp. 1346–7
15. Sheean, *Between the Thunder and the Sun*, p. 54
16. Gilbert, *Churchill V*, p. 1067

17. WSC, *The Second World War I: The Gathering Storm*, p. 357
18. Maze Papers. Quoted in Gilbert, *Companion V: 3*, p. 1591
19. Balsan, *The Glitter and the Gold*, p. 227
20. Ibid.
21. Maze Papers. Quoted in Gilbert, *Companion V: 3*, p. 1592
22. From the recollections of Det. Inspector W.H. Thompson (Churchill's bodyguard, September 1939–May 1945; married Mary Shearburn as his second wife). Quoted in Gilbert, *Companion V: 3*, p. 1592

CHAPTER EIGHT

1. Churchill Papers: 2/366; Gilbert, *Companion V: 3*, p. 1612
2. Letter from Dr Brés to WSC, 5 March 1940. Churchill Papers: 2/394; Gilbert, *Companion V: 3*, p. 1341
3. WSC, *The Second World War IV: The Hinge of Fate*, p. 621
4. Ibid. p. 622
5. Account of the expedition to Marrakech largely taken from Pawle, *The War and Colonel Warden*, pp. 226–7
6. Lord Moran, diary entry for 24 January 1943. Moran, *Winston Churchill: The Struggle for Survival 1940–1965*, p. 83
7. Mary Soames's diary, 8 July 1945
8. Colville, *The Fringes of Power*, p. 610
9. Ibid.
10. WSC, *The Second World War VI: Triumph and Tragedy*, p. 583
11. Sarah Churchill, *A Thread in the Tapestry*, p. 88
12. Spencer-Churchill Papers. Quoted in Gilbert, *Churchill VIII*, p. 134
13. Ibid.
14. Sarah Churchill, *A Thread in the Tapestry*, p. 91
15. Sarah Churchill to CSC, 3 September 1945. Spencer-Churchill Papers; Sarah Churchill, *A Thread in the Tapestry*, p. 91
16. Sarah Churchill, *A Thread in the Tapestry*, p. 92
17. Recollections of Field Marshal Lord Alexander of Tunis, in conversation with Martin Gilbert. Gilbert, *Churchill VIII*, p. 142
18. Sarah Churchill to CSC, 8 September 1945. Mary Soames Papers; Sarah Churchill, *A Thread in the Tapestry*, pp. 94–5
19. Sarah Churchill, *A Thread in the Tapestry*, pp. 95–8
20. Churchill Papers: 1/41; Gilbert *Churchill VIII*, p. 140
21. WSC to Mary Soames, 10 September 1945. Mary Soames Papers; Gilbert, *Churchill VIII*, p. 144
22. WSC to CSC, 18 September 1945. Spencer-Churchill Papers: Gilbert, *Churchill VIII*, p. 149
23. Ibid.
24. Ibid.
25. WSC to CSC, 24 September 1945. Spencer-Churchill Papers; Gilbert *Churchill VIII*, p. 152
26. Recollections of Col. Wathen (Commander of the Genoa Sub-Area). Gilbert, *Churchill VIII*, p. 152n
27. WSC to CSC, 24 September 1945. Spencer-Churchill Papers; Gilbert, *Churchill VIII*, p. 154
28. Ibid.

CHAPTER NINE

1. Lady Diana Cooper to Conrad Russell, 12 and 13 November 1945. Letters published in the *Spectator*, 23 May 1987
2. WSC to Robert Southon, 5 January 1946. Churchill Papers: 1/30; Gilbert, *Churchill VIII*, pp. 176–7

3. Mary Soames to WSC, 1 January 1946. Mary Soames Papers; Gilbert *Churchill VIII*, p. 177
4. CSC to Mary Soames, 18 January 1946. Mary Soames Papers
5. CSC to Mary Soames, 22 January 1946. Mary Soames Papers
6. CSC to Mary Soames, 27 January 1946. Mary Soames Papers
7. Ibid.
8. Mary Soames's diary, 15 June 1946
9. WSC to Alanbrooke, September 1946. Churchill Papers: 4/196; Gilbert, *Churchill VIII*, p. 262
10. WSC to Willy Sax, 16 October 1946. Churchill Papers
11. Mary Soames's diary, 6 September 1946
12. Ibid.
13. WSC, Zurich University, 19 September 1946
14. Mary Soames's diary, 27 September 1946
15. WSC to his grandson Winston Churchill, 5 January 1947. Churchill Papers: 1/42
16. Professor Thomas Bodkin, 'Churchill the Artist' in Eade (ed.), *Churchill By His Contemporaries*, p. 290
17. WSC to Sir Alfred Munnings, KCVO, 8 May 1949. Churchill Papers: 2/163
18. WSC to CSC, 18 December 1947. Spencer-Churchill Papers: Gilbert, *Churchill VIII*, pp. 380–1
19. Sarah Churchill to CSC, 16 December 1947. Mary Soames Papers
20. WSC to CSC, 24 December 1947. Spencer-Churchill Papers; Gilbert, *Churchill VIII*, p. 385
21. Ibid.

CHAPTER TEN
1. 'Chartwell Bulletin', 18 April 1950. Gilbert, *Churchill VIII*, p. 524
2. Jock Colville's diary, 2 May 1948. Colville, *The Fringes of Power*
3. WSC to *The Times* (unsent letter), 7 July 1946. Churchill Papers: 2/145; Gilbert, *Churchill VIII*, p. 246
4. WSC to Col. the Hon. J. J. Astor, 28 August 1937
5. Lady Margaret Myddelton to Mary Soames, 9 September 1989. Mary Soames Papers
6. Ibid.
7. WSC to Col. the Hon. J. J. Astor, 10 June 1948
8. Ibid.
9. Mary Soames's diary, 21 August 1948
10. Ibid., 24 August 1948
11. Graebner, *My Dear Mr Churchill*, p. 92
12. Professor Thomas Bodkin, 'Churchill the Artist' in Eade (ed.), *Churchill By His Contemporaries*, p. 289–90
13. WSC to Oswald Birley, MC, 28 June 1949. Churchill Papers: 2/160
14. WSC telegram to Walter Graebner, 6 August 1949. Churchill Papers: 1/77
15. Graebner, *My Dear Mr Churchill*, p. 73
16. WSC telegram to Bryce Nairn, 19 November 1949. Churchill Papers: 1/81; Gilbert, *Churchill VIII*, p. 498

CHAPTER ELEVEN
1. Brendan Bracken to Lord Beaverbrook, 10 January 1950. Beaverbrook Papers
2. WSC to CSC, 18 April 1950. Spencer-Churchill Papers; Gilbert, *Churchill VIII*, p. 523
3. WSC telegram to CSC, 1 January 1951. Churchill Papers: 1/47; Gilbert, *Churchill VIII*, p. 582
4. Graebner, *My Dear Mr Churchill*, pp. 80–1
5. Ibid.
6. Ibid.
7. WSC to Willy Sax, 24 January 1951. Churchill Papers: 2/176; Gilbert, *Churchill VIII*, p. 588

8. Professor Thomas Bodkin, 'Churchill the Artist' in Eade (ed.), *Churchill By his Contemporaries*, p. 293
9. Rothenstein, *Time's Thievish Progress*, p. 128. Churchill Papers: 2/175; Gilbert, *Churchill VIII*, p. 1153
10. Cowles, *An Artist's Journey*, p. 62

CHAPTER TWELVE
1. WSC to CSC, 25 March 1951. Spencer-Churchill Papers; Gilbert, *Churchill VIII*, p. 600
2. Ibid.
3. Rothenstein, *Mr Churchill the Artist*, p. 76
4. Cowles, *An Artist's Journey*, p. 62
5. Princess Margaret to WSC, 6 March 1951. Churchill Papers: 2/173; Gilbert, *Churchill VIII*, p. 598
6. Queen Elizabeth the Queen Mother to WSC, November 1952. Gilbert, *Churchill VIII*, p. 772
7. WSC to President Truman, 18 June 1951. Squerryes Lodge Archives; Gilbert, *Churchill VIII*, p. 615
8. President Truman to WSC, 28 June 1951. Squerryes Lodge Archives; Gilbert, *Churchill VIII*, p. 615
9. WSC to CSC, 3 August 1951. Churchill Papers: 1/49; Gilbert, *Churchill VIII*, p. 628

CHAPTER THIRTEEN
1. Recollections of Christopher Soames, in conversation with Mary Soames
2. Gilbert, *Churchill VIII*, p. 724
3. WSC broadcast, 7 February 1952
4. Colville, *The Fringes of Power*, p. 664
5. Coward, *Future Indefinite*, p. 50
6. Payne and Morley (eds), *The Noël Coward Diaries*, p. 207. Diary entry for 15 January 1953
7. Colville, *The Fringes of Power*, p. 647
8. Official Bulletin, 26 June 1953
9. WSC to CSC, 21 September 1953. Spencer-Churchill Papers; Gilbert, *Churchill VIII*, p. 888
10. Mary Soames's diary, 22 September 1953
11. WSC telegram to CSC, 23 September 1953. Churchill Papers: 1/50; Gilbert, *Churchill VIII*, p. 889
12. WSC to CSC, 25 September 1953. Spencer-Churchill Papers; Gilbert, *Churchill VIII*, p. 890
13. Soames, *Clementine Churchill*, p. 439

CHAPTER FOURTEEN
1. Oscar Nemon typescript sent to Bartlett Watt
2. Coombs, *Churchill: His Paintings*, p. 11
3. Oscar Nemon, to WSC, 5 May 1955. Churchill Papers: 2/195; Gilbert, *Churchill VIII*, p. 1147
4. Oscar Nemon to Dr J. Siegenberg of Edmonton, Alberta, 15 March 1985
5. Cowles, *An Artist's Journey*, p. 33–8 (tape-recorded interview)
6. Ibid.
7. Ibid.
8. Graham Sutherland, OM, to Lord Birkenhead. Birkenhead, *Churchill 1874–1922*, p. 515
9. Recollections of CSC, in conversation with Mary Soames
10. Lord Normanbrook in Wheeler-Bennett, *Action This Day: Working With Churchill*, pp. 44–5
11. Mary Soames's diary, 19 March 1955
12. *Hansard*, 1 March 1955; Gilbert, *Churchill VIII*, p. 1100
13. Mary Soames's diary, 6 April 1955

14. Moran, *Winston Churchill: The Struggle for Survival 1940–1965*, p. 1133
15. Ibid.
16. Rothenstein, *Time's Thievish Progress*, p. 137
17. Ibid. p. 140
18. Ibid. p. 137
19. Churchill Papers. From a draft by John Rothenstein for his piece 'Mr Churchill the Artist', later to be published in *Churchill: A Tribute by various hands, on his Eightieth Birthday*
20. Ibid.
21. Rothenstein, *Time's Thievish Progress*, p. 144
22. CSC to Lord Beaverbrook, 17 August 1952. Beaverbrook Papers

CHAPTER FIFTEEN
1. Kenneth Rose to Mary Soames; an extract from his diary recalling a conversation with Lord Butler
2. WSC, *Painting as a Pastime*, p. 13
3. CSC to WSC, January 1958. Churchill Papers: 1/55; Gilbert, *Churchill VIII*, p. 1259
4. CSC to Wendy Reves, 20 January 1958. Reves Papers; Gilbert, *Churchill VIII*, p. 1258
5. WSC to CSC, 22 January 1958. Spencer-Churchill Papers; Gilbert, *Churchill VIII*, p. 1258
6. WSC to CSC, 23 January 1958. Spencer-Churchill Papers; Gilbert, *Churchill VIII*, p. 1259
7. Sir John Colville to Martin Gilbert, 12 November 1986. Quoted in Gilbert, *Churchill VIII*, p. 1283
8. CSC to Mary Soames, 28 January 1959. Mary Soames Papers
9. CSC to WSC, 25 March 1959. Churchill Papers: 1/135; Gilbert, *Churchill VIII*, p. 1288
10. President Eisenhower to WSC, 26 May 1959. Churchill Papers: 2/217; Gilbert, *Churchill VIII*, p. 1296
11. Soames, *Clementine Churchill*, p. 469
12. Queen Elizabeth II to WSC, 11 May 1960. Squerryes Lodge Archive; Gilbert, *Churchill VIII*, p. 1313
13. WSC, *Painting as a Pastime*, p. 16
14. Ibid. p. 13

Select Bibliography

Ashley, Maurice, *Churchill as Historian*, Secker (London) 1968

Balsan, Consuelo Vanderbilt, *The Glitter and the Gold*, Heinemann (London) 1953

Baron, Dr Wendy, *Sickert*, Phaidon (London) 1973

Birkenhead, Earl of, *Churchill 1874–1922*, Harrap (London) 1989

Churchill, Sarah, *A Thread in the Tapestry*, Deutsch (London) 1967

Churchill, Winston S., *Painting as a Pastime*, Odhams (London) 1948

——*The Second World War* (6 volumes), Cassell (London) 1948–54

——*Thoughts and Adventures*, (London) 1932

Colville, John, *The Fringes of Power: Downing Street Diaries 1939–1955*, Hodder & Stoughton (London) 1985

Coombs, David, *Churchill: His Paintings*, Hamish Hamilton (London) 1967

Coward, Noël, *Future Indefinite*, Heinemann (London) 1954

Cowles, Fleur, *An Artist's Journey*, Collins (London) 1988

Eade, Charles (ed.), *Churchill By His Contemporaries*, Random Century (London) 1953

Forbes-Robertson, Diana, *Maxine*, Hamish Hamilton (London) 1964

Gilbert, Martin, *Winston S. Churchill* (volumes III–VIII), Heinemann (London) 1971–88

——*Companion Volumes* (III–V), Heinemann (London) 1972–82

Goodman, Jean *What A Go! The Life of Alfred Munnings*, Collins (London) 1988

Graebner, Walter, *My Dear Mr Churchill*, Michael Joseph (London) 1965

Lavery, John, *The Life of a Painter*, Cassell (London) 1940

Marsh, Edward, *A Number of People*, Heinemann (London) 1939

Maze, Paul, *A Frenchman in Khaki*, Heinemann (London) 1934

Moran, Lord, *Winston Churchill: The Struggle for Survival 1940–1965*, Constable (London) 1966

Pawle, Gerald, *The War and Colonel Warden*, Harrap (London) 1963

Payne, Graham and Morley, Sheridan (eds), *The Noël Coward Diaries*, Weidenfeld & Nicolson (London) 1982

Quennell, Peter, *The Wanton Chase*, Collins (London) 1980

Rothenstein, John, *Time's Thievish Progress: Autobiography III*, Cassell (London) 1960

Sheean, Vincent, *Between the Thunder and the Sun*, Macmillan (London) 1943

Soames, Mary, *Clementine Churchill*, Cassell (London) 1979

Steen, Marguerite, *Pier Glass: More Autobiography*, Longman (London) 1968

Wheeler-Bennett, Sir John (ed.) *Action This Day: Working with Churchill*, Macmillan (London) 1968

Woods, Frederick, *A Bibliography of the Works of Sir Winston Churchill* (revised edn), Kaye & Ward (London) 1969 (first published by Nicholas Vane, 1963)

Index